Grade
9

Analytic
Geometry

D1709419

ISBN: 978-1-77149-361-1

Smart High School Series – MathSmart Grade 9 (Analytic Geometry) is designed to help students build solid foundations in high-school-level math and excel in key math concepts.

This workbook covers the key concepts of analytic geometry in the Mathematics curriculum, including topics on:

- Linear and Non-linear Relations
- Properties of Slopes
- Characteristics of Relations
- Forms of Linear Equations: $y = mx + b$ and $Ax + By + C = 0$

This workbook contains three chapters, with each chapter covering a math topic. Different concepts within the topic are each introduced by a "Key Ideas" section and examples are provided to give students an opportunity to consolidate their understanding. The "Try these!" section allows students to ease into the concept with basic skill questions, and is followed by the "Practice" section with questions that gradually increase in difficulty to help students consolidate the concept they have learned. Useful hints are provided to guide students along and help them grasp the essential math concepts. In addition, a handy summary of the concepts learned is included at the end of each chapter along with space for students to make their own notes for quick and easy reference whenever needed.

A quiz at the end of each chapter as well as a final test are provided to recapitulate the concepts and skills students have learned in the book. The questions are classified into four categories to help students evaluate their own learning. Below are the four categories:

- Knowledge and Understanding
- Application
- Communication
- Thinking

This approach to testing practice effectively prepares students for the Math examination in school.

Additionally, the "Math IRL" sections throughout the book demonstrate the use of the investigated math topics in real-life scenarios to help students recognize the ubiquity and function of math in everyday settings. Bonus online resources can also be accessed by scanning the included QR codes.

At the end of this workbook is an answer key that provides thorough solutions with the crucial steps clearly presented to help students develop an understanding of the correct strategies and approaches to arrive at the solutions.

MathSmart Grade 9 (Analytic Geometry) will undoubtedly reinforce students' math skills and strengthen the conceptual foundation needed as a prerequisite for exploring mathematics further in their secondary programs.

Contents

Chapter 1: Investigating Relations

1.1   The Cartesian Plane 4

1.2   Determining the Slope of a Line 8

1.3   Properties of Slopes 14

1.4 x- and y-intercepts 20

1.5   Linear Relations and Non-linear Relations 26

      Quiz 1 32

Chapter 2: Forms of Linear Equations

2.1   Slope-intercept Form: $y = mx + b$ (1) 38

2.2   Slope-intercept Form: $y = mx + b$ (2) 44

2.3   Standard Form: $Ax + By + C = 0$ 48

2.4   Vertical Lines and Horizontal Lines: $x = a$, $y = b$ 54

2.5   Equation of a Line 58

2.6   Relating Linear Equations 64

      Quiz 2 68

Chapter 3: Interpreting Linear Equations

3.1   Points of Intersection 74

3.2   Parallel Lines and Perpendicular Lines 80

3.3   Applications of Linear Relations (1) 86

3.4   Applications of Linear Relations (2) 92

      Quiz 3 96

Final Test 102

Answers 109

Investigating Relations

1.1 The Cartesian Plane

Key Ideas

The Cartesian plane, also known as the xy-plane, has two perpendicular lines that intersect at the origin. The horizontal line is called the x-axis and the vertical line is called the y-axis. The axes cut the plane into four sections called quadrants. The quadrants are labelled I, II, III, and IV.

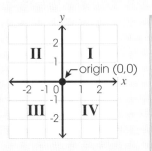

Coordinates of a Point (x,y)

Each point on the plane can be identified by an ordered pair of numbers in the form of (x,y). These are called coordinates. The first number is the x-coordinate and the second number is the y-coordinate.

Examples

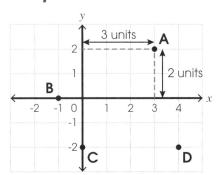

No. of quadrants on the plane: __4__

Point in Quadrant IV: __D__

Point on the x-axis: __B__

Point on the y-axis: __C__

x-coordinate
y-coordinate

Coordinates of A: __(3,2)__

Complete the Cartesian plane. Then answer the questions.

Try these!

①

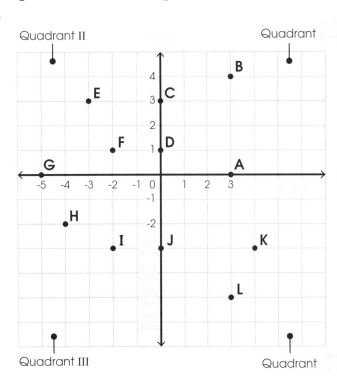

a. Points on the x-axis: _____

b. Points on the y-axis: _____

c. Coordinates of the points:

A(,)   B(,)

C(,)   D(,)

E(,)   F(,)

G(,)   H(,)

I(,)   J(,)

K(,)   L(,)

Find the coordinates of the points on the plane and plot the points. Then write the answers.

② a. Coordinates of the points:

A _____   B _____

C _____   D _____

E _____   F _____

G _____   H _____

I _____   J _____

K _____   L _____

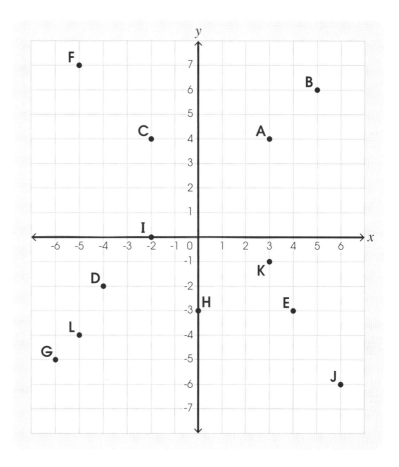

b. Plot the points.

   M(6,2)   N(3,-4)

   O(-3,-3)   P(1,-4)

   Q(-5,4)   R(1,3)

   S(-1,0)   T(0,-5)

c. Points that have "3" as their x-coordinate: _____

d. Points that have "-4" as their y-coordinate: _____

e. Points that lie on the x-axis: _____

f. Points that lie on the y-axis: _____

g. Points that are in Quadrant II: _____

h. Points that are in Quadrant IV: _____

i.

Points (x,y)	Quadrant I	Quadrant II	Quadrant III	Quadrant IV
x-coordinate (positive/negative)		negative		
y-coordinate (positive/negative)		positive		

Plot the points and answer the questions.

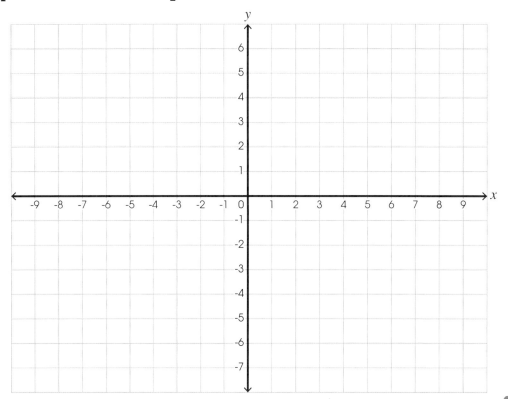

③ Plot the points on the plane.

A(-1,-1)   B(2,6)   C(5,-2)   D(1,-2)
E(-5,6)   F(2,1)   G(2,-6)   H(-2,6)
I(-6,-7)   J(-7,1)   K(7,6)   L(-1,-7)

④ What is the distance between

a. Points B and G?   _____

b. Points E and H?   _____

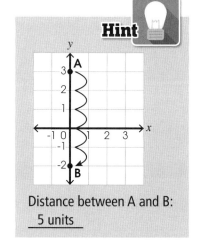

Distance between A and B:
    5 units

⑤ List the points by quadrant. Add one point to each quadrant to create the specified quadrilateral. Then write the coordinates of the new point.

Quadrant I (square)	Quadrant II (kite)	Quadrant III (rectangle)	Quadrant IV (parallelogram)
_____	_____	_____	_____
_____	_____	_____	_____
_____	_____	_____	_____
_____	_____	_____	_____

Answer the questions.

⑥ Connect each set of points in order. What letter do you see?
- Set A: (1,3), (1,1), (2,1)
- Set B: (-1,3), (1,-1), (3,3)
- Set C: (-3,5), (1,5), (-1,-3), (3,-3)

⑦ Connect each set of points. Which set forms an isosceles triangle?
- Set A: (-2,6), (-2,4), (5,5)
- Set B: (2,1), (6,1), (4,-5)
- Set C: (-3,1), (-3,-3), (-8,-3)

⑧ Consider each set of points below.
- Set A: (-8,7), (-6,1), (-5,3), (-4,1), (-2,7)
- Set B: (4,0), (4,4), (6,0), (6,4)
- Set C: (4,-6), (6,-2), (7,0), (9,4)
- Set D: (-8,-1), (-7,-2), (-5,-4), (-4,-5), (-2,-7)
- Set E: (3,0), (1,0), (-3,0), (-4,0), (-6,0)
- Set F: (0,4), (0,2), (0,-1), (0,-4), (0,-5)

a. Plot the points on a Cartesian plane.
b. Connect the points in order. Describe what you see.
c. Write the coordinates of two more points that belong to each set.

⑨ Describe the line that connects two points which have the same x-coordinate.

⑩ Describe the line that connects two points which have the same y-coordinate.

⑪ What is common in the coordinates of all the points that lie on the x-axis? On the y-axis?

⑫ The vertices of a parallelogram are at (-2,-2), (-4,-2), (-4,-6), and (-6,-6); the vertices of its image are at (2,-2), (4,-2), (4,-6), and (6,-6). Was the parallelogram translated, reflected, or rotated?

⑬ Points M(-3,2) and N(-3,-2) are vertices of a square. If the square lies in all four quadrants, what are the coordinates of the other two vertices?

M A T H   I R L

In Mathematics, the Cartesian coordinate system allows us to specify a unique location by a pair of coordinates. However, the use of coordinates for positioning is not limited to Mathematics. In Geography, a geographic coordinate system (GCS) is used to indicate positions on Earth's surface. The latitude and longitude are geographic coordinates that specify the position of a point on Earth. Scan this QR code to learn more about the components of GCS.

Chapter 1

1.2 Determining the Slope of a Line

Key Ideas

The slope is the measure of the steepness of a line. It is the ratio of the vertical distance (also called the rise) and the horizontal distance (also called the run) between two points on the line. The vertical distance is the difference of the two points' y-values and the horizontal distance is the difference of their x-values. The slope of a line is commonly denoted by m.

Slope of a Line

$$m = \frac{\text{rise}}{\text{run}} = \frac{y_2 - y_1}{x_2 - x_1}$$

Examples

Find the slopes of the lines.

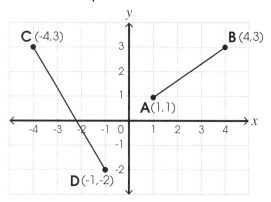

- Slope of line segment AB:

$$m = \frac{3 - 1}{4 - 1} \begin{array}{l} \leftarrow y_2 - y_1 \text{ (difference in } y\text{-values)} \\ \leftarrow x_2 - x_1 \text{ (difference in } x\text{-values)} \end{array}$$

$$= \frac{2}{3}$$

- Slope of line segment CD:

$$m = \frac{(-2) - 3}{(-1) - (-4)} = -\frac{5}{3}$$

Find the slopes of the line segments.

Try these!

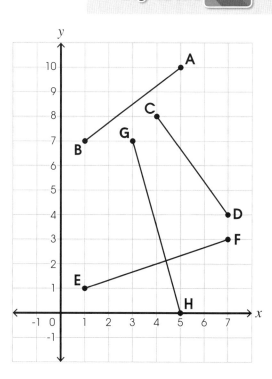

① Line AB

$$m = \frac{7 - \underline{\hspace{1cm}}}{1 - \underline{\hspace{1cm}}} \begin{array}{l} \leftarrow y_2 - y_1 \\ \leftarrow x_2 - x_1 \end{array}$$

$$= \underline{\hspace{1cm}}$$

② Line CD

$$m = \frac{4 - \underline{\hspace{1cm}}}{7 - \underline{\hspace{1cm}}}$$

$$= -\underline{\hspace{1cm}}$$

③ Line EF

$$m = \frac{3 - \underline{\hspace{1cm}}}{\underline{\hspace{1cm}} - \underline{\hspace{1cm}}}$$

$$= \underline{\hspace{1cm}}$$

④ Line GH

$$m = \frac{0 - \underline{\hspace{1cm}}}{\underline{\hspace{1cm}} - \underline{\hspace{1cm}}}$$

$$= -\underline{\hspace{1cm}}$$

Find the slopes of the line segments with the given points on the grid.

⑤

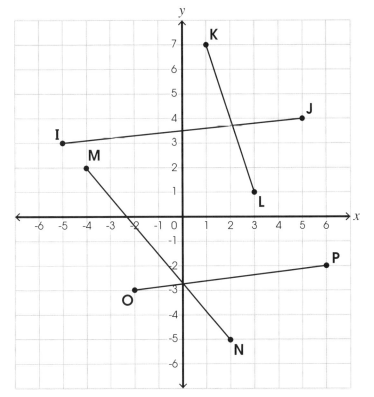

a. Line IJ   b. Line KL   c. Line MN   d. Line OP

$$m = \frac{\quad - \quad}{\quad - \quad}$$

$$= \frac{\quad}{\quad}$$

Find the slopes of the line segments with the given points. Show your work.

⑥ (2,0) (4,9)   ⑦ (-1,3) (4,5)   ⑧ (6,-3) (4,-1)

⑨ (-2,-4) (3,-1)   ⑩ (4,1) (5,-6)   ⑪ (0,-3) (-2,2)

Find the slopes of the line segments with the given points. Then answer the questions.

Hint

$\overline{AB}$ denotes the line segment joining Point A and Point B.

m_{AB} denotes the slope of $\overline{AB}$.

⑫

A(6,3)   B(4,-6)   C(3,-1)   D(-2,2)

E(0,8)   F(-4,-4)   G(0,-5)   H(2,1)

a. m_{AB} = _____ = _____

b. m_{AD} = _____ = _____

c. m_{BC} = _____ = _____   d. m_{CF} = _____ = _____

e. m_{FH} = _____ = _____   f. m_{GA} = _____ = _____

g. Should the slopes of $\overline{DH}$ and $\overline{HD}$ be the same? Explain.

_____

_____

h. Point C lies on $\overline{AG}$. Are the slopes of $\overline{AG}$ and $\overline{AC}$ the same? Explain.

_____

_____

i.

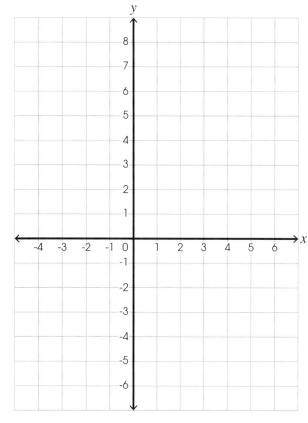

Plot the points. Determine two line segments that have the same slope as each given line segment. Then determine the slopes.

slope
• m_{AG} = _____ = _____

slope
• m_{BE} = _____ = _____

slope
• m_{BF} = _____ = _____

slope
• m_{EF} = _____ = _____

Find the slopes of the lines. Show your work.

⑬

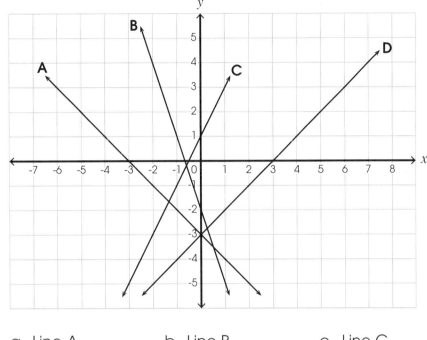

Hint

Any two points on a line can be used to find the slope. For accuracy, use points that have integers as their coordinates.

a. Line A   b. Line B   c. Line C   d. Line D

Determine whether the given points are collinear and write "=" or "≠" in the circle. Then fill in the blanks.

⑭   A(0,-1)   B(1,2)   C(-1,-4)

m_{AB} = _____ = _____

m_{BC} = _____ = _____

m_{AB} ◯ m_{BC}

Hint

If three or more points lie on the same line, then they are collinear. The slopes of the line segments of any two collinear points must be equal.

The points are _____ .
                    collinear/not collinear

⑮   L(-1,-6)   M(-4,0)   N(-6,4)   ⑯   R(2,-3)   S(-1,10)   T(0,7)

The points are _____ .   The points are _____ .

Find the missing coordinates of each point with the given slope of the line. Show your work.

⑰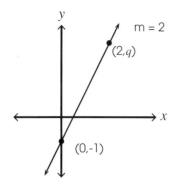

$m = \dfrac{y_2 - y_1}{x_2 - x_1}$ ← slope formula

$2 = \dfrac{q - (-1)}{2 - 0}$ ← Substitute values into the slope formula.

$2 = \dfrac{q + 1}{2}$ ← Solve for q.

$\quad = \quad$

$q = \qquad$ ← value of q

Hint

To find the unknown coordinates, substitute both points and the given slope into the slope formula. Then solve.

⑱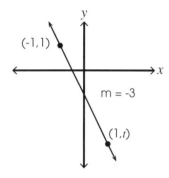

⑲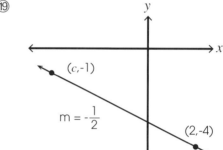

⑳ E(1,e)   F(3,-7) $m_{EF} = -5$

㉑ U(u,-2)   V(-3,-8) $m_{UV} = \dfrac{2}{3}$

㉒ I(4,-2)   J(j,8) $m_{IJ} = -\dfrac{5}{4}$

㉓ G(g,-5)   H(-8,-11) $m_{GH} = \dfrac{3}{2}$

Answer the questions.

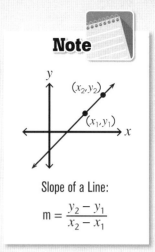

Note

Slope of a Line:

$$m = \frac{y_2 - y_1}{x_2 - x_1}$$

㉔ Find the slope of the line that passes through each pair of points.

a. (4,-1) and (0,-5)

b. (-5,1) and (4,-8)

c. (-1,4) and (3,-8)

d. (0,3) and (5,5)

e. (5,2) and (2,3)

f. (-3,-2) and (6,4)

g. (-1,-6) and (-5,-3)

h. (3,2) and (9,-3)

i. (7,-2) and (-3,-5)

j. (-1,0) and (4,3)

㉕ The point (2,4) lies on a line with a slope of -1. What are the coordinates of the point on the line that has an x-coordinate of 7?

㉖ The point (-3,7) lies on a line with a slope of -3. What are the coordinates of the point on the line that has a y-coordinate of -2?

㉗ Find the unknown values with the given slopes of the lines and coordinates of the points.

a. A(-5,-3), B(9,b), $m_{AB} = \dfrac{2}{7}$

b. C(3,5), D(-2,d), $m_{CD} = \dfrac{8}{5}$

c. E(e,-5), F(2,-8), $m_{EF} = -\dfrac{3}{2}$

d. G(-4,3), H(h,-1), $m_{GH} = -\dfrac{2}{5}$

㉘ Consider the sets of points below.

- Set A: (-2,3), (0,-2), (2,-7)
- Set B: (-1,6), (4,-3), (5,1)
- Set C: (-8,4), (9,0), (2,-3)
- Set D: (-5,-5), (5,13), (0,4)

Determine which sets of points are collinear without graphing. Explain how you know.

㉙ Lisa says, "When applying the slope formula, the order of the points does not matter, meaning $m = \dfrac{y_2 - y_1}{x_2 - x_1} = \dfrac{y_1 - y_2}{x_1 - x_2}$." Is she correct? Give an example.

㉚ Scott thinks that if $\overline{AB}$ and $\overline{CD}$ have the same slope, then Points A, B, C, and D must lie on the same line. Is he correct? Give an example.

㉛ Aaron says, "Consider Points A, B, C, D, and E. If Points A, B, and C are collinear, and Points C, D, and E are collinear, then m_{AD} and m_{BE} are the same." Is he correct? Explain.

Chapter 1

Key Ideas

The value of the slope of a line determines the properties of the line. These properties include the steepness and direction of the line.

- **steepness:**
  the greater the magnitude* of the slope value, the steeper the line; the lesser the slope value, the gentler the slope of the line

- **direction:**
  a line rising from the left to the right has a positive slope value; a line falling from the left to the right has a negative value

*The magnitude of a number is its distance from zero. For example, the magnitude of 5 is 5 and the magnitude of -2 is 2.

Examples

Match the slope that best represents the line.

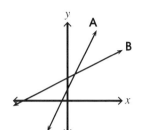

m = 2	m = $\frac{1}{2}$
(greater; steeper slope)	(lesser; gentler slope)
__Line A__	__Line B__

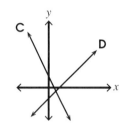

m = -2	m = 1
(negative; falls to right)	(positive; rises to right)
__Line C__	__Line D__

Draw lines to match the lines with their slopes.

Try these!

①

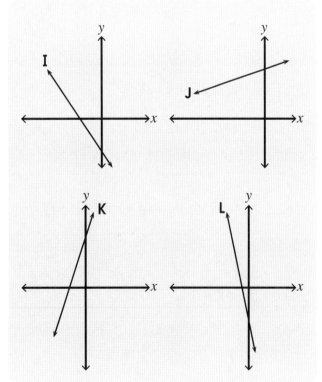

a. Line I •

b. Line J •

c. Line K •

d. Line L •

Slope

- m = -5
  greatest magnitude (steepest); negative (falls to right)

- m = $\frac{1}{3}$
  least magnitude (gentlest); positive (rises to right)

- m = 3
  positive

- m = -$\frac{3}{2}$
  negative

Find the slope of the line with the given points. Graph it. Then answer the questions.

② A(7,5) B(4,-4)

③ M(-7,1) N(-5,-3)

④ I(9,4) J(8,-4)

⑤ C(-3,3) D(3,-3)

⑥ S(-9,-5) T(-2,-3)

⑦ E(1,5) F(2,-4)

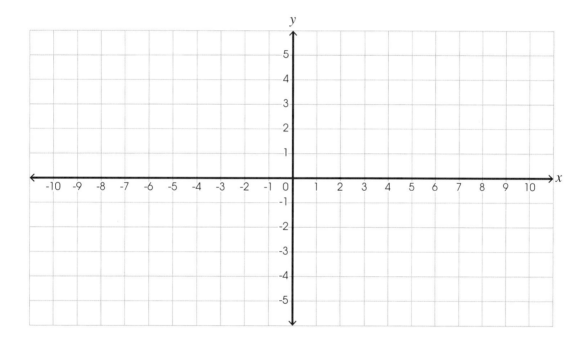

⑧ Consider the lines above.

a. Do all the lines that have positive slopes rise to the right?

_____

b. Do all the lines that have negative slopes fall to the right?

_____

c. Which line has the greatest magnitude? Is it the steepest?

_____

d. Which line has the least magnitude? Does it have the gentlest slope?

_____

Find the slopes of the line segments and answer the questions.

⑨

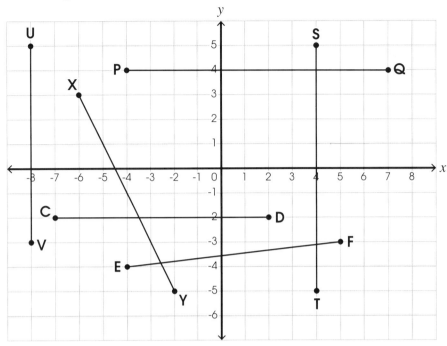

Hint

Any horizontal line has a slope of 0.

no rise

$m = \dfrac{0}{run} = 0$

Any vertical line has a slope that is undefined.

no run

$m = \dfrac{rise}{0} = undefined$

a. $\overline{CD}$

b. $\overline{EF}$

c. $\overline{PQ}$

d. $\overline{ST}$

e. $\overline{UV}$

f. $\overline{XY}$

⑩ What are the slopes of the horizontal lines? Is it possible for a line to be not horizontal and have a slope of 0? Explain.

_____

⑪ What are the slopes of the vertical lines? Is it possible for a line to be vertical and have a slope of a numerical value? Explain.

_____

Find the slopes of each pair of lines. Then answer the questions.

⑫ Parallel Lines

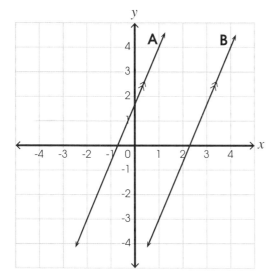

⑬ Perpendicular Lines

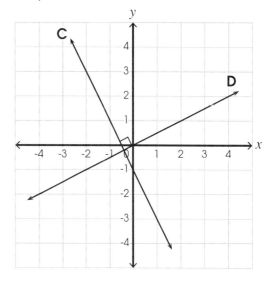

⑭ Compare the slopes of the parallel lines. What do you find?

_____

⑮ Compare the slopes of the perpendicular lines. What do you find?

_____

Find the slopes of the parallel lines and perpendicular lines and fill in the blanks with the correct line segments.

⑯ $m_{PQ} = 3$

a. $\overline{PQ} // \overline{RS}$

$m_{RS} = $ _____

b. $\overline{PQ} \perp \overline{UV}$

$m_{UV} = $ _____

⑰ $m_{EF} = -\dfrac{1}{4}$

a. $\overline{EF} // \overline{AB}$

$m_{AB} = $ _____

b. $\overline{EF} \perp \overline{CD}$

$m_{CD} = $ _____

c. $m_{IJ} = -\dfrac{1}{4}$

$\overline{IJ} // $ _____

d. $m_{PQ} = 4$

$\overline{PQ} \perp $ _____

Hint

Parallel lines have the same slope.

If $\overline{AB} // \overline{CD}$,   ⎯ parallel to

then $m_{AB} = m_{CD}$.

Perpendicular lines have slopes that are negative reciprocals of each other.

If $\overline{AB} \perp \overline{CD}$,   ⎯ perpendicular to

then $m_{AB} = -\dfrac{1}{m_{CD}}$.

Fill in the blanks and answer the questions.

⑱ Consider m as the slope of a line.

    a. If m < 0, the line _____ to the right.

    b. If m > 0, the line _____ to the right.

    c. If m = 0, the line is _____ .

    d. If m = undefined, the line is _____ .

    e. Describe the slope of each line numerically.

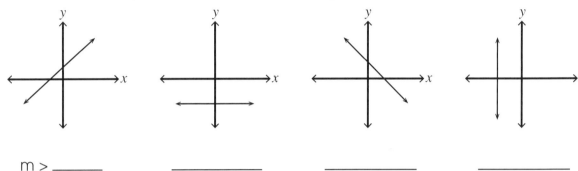

        m > _____   _____   _____   _____

⑲ Consider m_{AB}, m_{CD}, and m_{EF} as the slopes of $\overline{AB}$, $\overline{CD}$, and $\overline{EF}$ respectively.

    a. If the magnitude of m_{AB} is greater than that of m_{CD}, then the steepness of $\overline{AB}$

       is _____ .

    b. If the magnitude of m_{AB} is lesser than that of m_{CD}, then the steepness of $\overline{AB}$ is

      _____ .

    c. If $m_{AB} = m_{CD}$, then the lines are _____ .

    d. If $m_{AB} = -\dfrac{1}{m_{EF}}$, then the lines are _____ .

    e. Write ">" or "<" in the circle.   f. Write the answers.

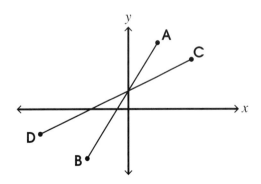

    magnitude ◯ magnitude
      of m_{AB} of m_{CD}

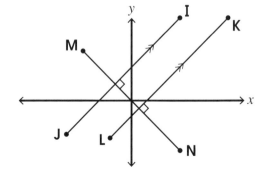

  • $\overline{IJ} \,/\!/\, \overline{KL}$ • $\overline{IJ} \perp \overline{MN}$

    $m_{IJ} =$ _____ $m_{IJ} =$ _____

Answer the questions.

⑳ Match the lines with the slopes.

- $m = 0$ • $m = \dfrac{1}{5}$ • $m = -\dfrac{3}{2}$ • $m = \dfrac{3}{2}$ • $m = -\dfrac{1}{4}$ • $m =$ undefined

a. 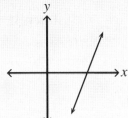   b. 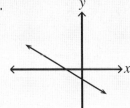   c.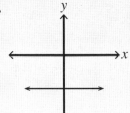

d. 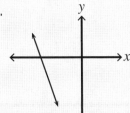   e. 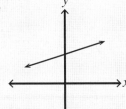   f.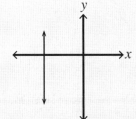

㉑ Consider each pair of points of a line segment. Answer the questions without graphing.

- A(2,8), B(-5,-6)
- E(-6,3), F(9,-2)
- C(2,-10), D(-4,8)
- G(-4,-1), H(8,8)

a. Find the slope of each line segment.

b. Describe the direction of each line segment.

c. Which line segment is the steepest? How do you know?

㉒ Consider $\overline{MN}$ and $\overline{OP}$ with the following sets of coordinates. Answer the questions without graphing.

- Set A: M(-1,-4), N(1,6), O(2,2), P(0,-8)
- Set B: M(2,9), N(-2,-7), O(8,4), P(-8,-8)
- Set C: M(6,7), N(-6,-1), O(-4,8), P(2,-1)

a. Find the slopes of the line segments in each set.

b. Which set has line segments that are parallel? Explain.

c. Which set has line segments that are perpendicular? Explain.

d. Which set has line segments that are neither parallel nor perpendicular?

㉓ What is the slope of a line that is perpendicular to a vertical line? Explain.

㉔ What is the slope of a line that is parallel to a horizontal line? Explain.

㉕ There are three line segments in a graph: $\overline{EF}$ // $\overline{GH}$ and $\overline{GH} \perp \overline{IJ}$. If $m_{EF} = \dfrac{2}{3}$, what is the slope of $\overline{IJ}$?

Chapter 1

Key Ideas

Any line, when extended, will cross the *x*-axis and/or the *y*-axis on the Cartesian plane.

The point where the line crosses the *x*-axis is called the *x*-intercept. It always has a *y*-coordinate of 0.

The point where the line crosses the *y*-axis is called the *y*-intercept. It always has an *x*-coordinate of 0.

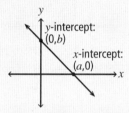

Any horizontal line has one *y*-intercept only and any vertical line has one *x*-intercept only.

Examples

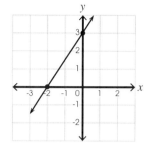

- *x*-intercept:
  (-2,0) ← lies on *x*-axis
- *y*-intercept:
  (0,3) ← lies on *y*-axis

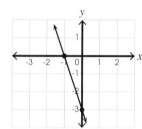

- *x*-intercept:
  (-1,0)
- *y*-intercept:
  (0,-3)

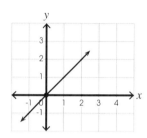

The coordinates of both the *x*-intercept and *y*-intercept are (0,0).

Try these!

Identify and mark the *x*- and *y*-intercepts of the lines. Then write their coordinates.

①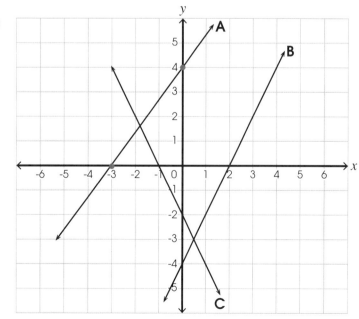

a. Line A
- *x*-intercept: (,0) ← lies on *x*-axis
- *y*-intercept: (0,   ) ← lies on *y*-axis

b. Line B
- *x*-intercept: (,0)
- *y*-intercept: (0,   )

c. Line C
- *x*-intercept: (,   )
- *y*-intercept: (,   )

Determine the coordinates of the *x*- and *y*-intercepts of each line. Then find the slope.

②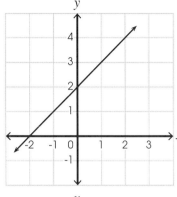

a. *x*-intercept: ([   ] ,0) ← 1st point

y-intercept: (0, [   ]) ← 2nd point

b. $m = \dfrac{\boxed{} - 0}{0 - \boxed{}}$

$= \boxed{}$

Hint

The *x*-intercept and *y*-intercept of a line are two points that lie on the line, so they can be used to find the slope. If the coordinates of the *x*- and *y*-intercepts are integers, then they are better suited than other points for finding the slope because the zero values help simplify the slope formula.

③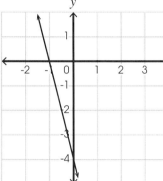

a. *x*-intercept: _____

y-intercept: _____

b. m = _____

= _____

④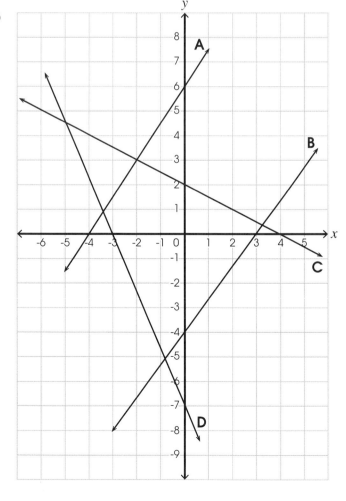

a. Line A

b. Line B

c. Line C

d. Line D

Draw each line with the given descriptions. Then find its slope.

⑤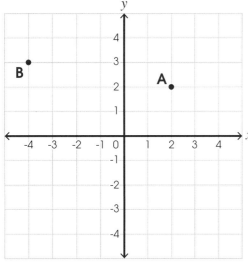

a. a line that passes through Point A and has an *x*-intercept of -3

b. a line that passes through Point B and has a *y*-intercept of -3

⑥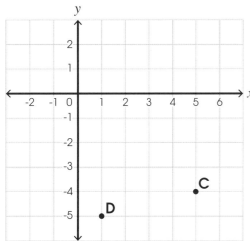

a. a line that passes through Point C and has an *x*-intercept of -1

b. a line that passes through Point D and has a *y*-intercept of -2

⑦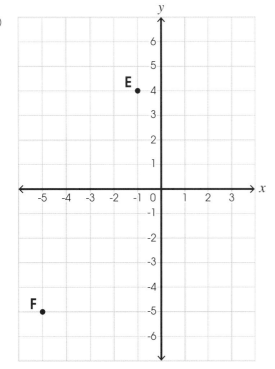

a. a line that passes through Point E and has a *y*-intercept of -1

b. a line that passes through Point F and has an *x*-intercept of -4

c. a line that has the same *x*-intercept as the line through Point F and the same *y*-intercept as the line through Point E

Find the x- and y-intercepts of each line with the given slope and point.

⑧ a line with a slope of 1 and passes through (2,4)

a. x-intercept:

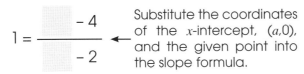

$$1 = \frac{\boxed{} - 4}{\boxed{} - 2} \quad \leftarrow$$ Substitute the coordinates of the x-intercept, $(a,0)$, and the given point into the slope formula.

$\boxed{} - 2 = -4 \quad \leftarrow$ Solve for a.

$a = \boxed{}$ x-intercept = _____

Hint

Use the slope formula to find the x- and y-intercepts. Recall that all x-intercepts have a y-coordinate of 0 and all y-intercepts have an x-coordinate of 0.

b. y-intercept:

$$1 = \frac{\boxed{} - 4}{\boxed{} - 2} \quad \leftarrow$$ Substitute the coordinates of the y-intercept, $(0,b)$, and the given point into the slope formula.

$\boxed{} - 4 = -2 \quad \leftarrow$ Solve for b.

$b = \boxed{}$ y-intercept = _____

⑨ a line with a slope of 3 and passes through (1,6)

a. Find the x-intercept.

x-intercept = _____

b. Find the y-intercept.

y-intercept = _____

⑩ a line with a slope of -2 and passes through (-1,-2)

a. Find the x-intercept.

x-intercept = _____

b. Find the y-intercept.

y-intercept = _____

Use the given slope and point to find the *x*- and *y*-intercepts of each line. Show your work.

⑪ $m = \dfrac{1}{2}$ (-4,-1)

⑫ $m = -\dfrac{2}{3}$ (6,-2)

⑬ $m = -\dfrac{5}{2}$ (-4,5)

Find the *x*- and *y*-intercepts of each line that passes through each pair of points. Show your work.

⑭   (3,3) (9,1)

Hint

First, find the slope using the two given points. Then use the slope and one of the two points to find the *x*- and *y*-intercepts.

⑮   (-5,1) (5,3)

⑯   (-8,1) (2,-4)

Answer the questions.

⑰ Find the slopes of the lines with the given x- and y-intercepts.

    a. x-intercept = -2   b. x-intercept = -5   c. x-intercept = 3

        y-intercept = -3 y-intercept = 2 y-intercept = -5

⑱ Find the coordinates of the x- and y-intercepts of the lines with the given descriptions.

    a. a slope of -2 and passes through (-3,8)

    b. a slope of $\frac{1}{5}$ and passes through (10,3)

    c. passes through (-9,8) and (-6,4)

    d. passes through (7,-3) and (-7,-9)

⑲ What is the y-intercept of a horizontal line that passes through (6,3)?

⑳ What is the x-intercept of a vertical line that passes through (-4,5)?

㉑ State whether each of the following is true or false.

    a. All straight lines have one x-intercept and one y-intercept.

    b. A line that has an x-intercept of 0 must also have a y-intercept of 0.

    c. Two lines are identical if they share the same x- and y-intercepts, for any value other than 0.

    d. A line with a positive x-intercept and a negative y-intercept has a positive slope.

    e. A line with a negative x-intercept and a negative y-intercept does not lie in Quadrant I.

    f. A line with an undefined slope must have a y-intercept.

㉒ For the lines with the given intercepts, list the quadrants the lines lie in.

    a. x-intercept = -3, y-intercept = 9

    b. x-intercept = 4, y-intercept = -1

    c. x-intercept = -2, no y-intercept

    d. no x-intercept, y-intercept = 6

㉓ The slope of any line can be found if its x- and y-intercepts are known. Is it true? Explain.

㉔ Consider a line that has the intercept at (0,0). How does knowing whether its slope is positive or negative help identify the quadrants that the line lies in? List the possible outcomes.

㉕ Describe the possible x- and y-intercepts of a line that lies in Quadrants I and IV by stating whether they are positive or negative.

Chapter 1

1.5 Linear Relations and Non-linear Relations

Key Ideas

A linear relation forms a straight line when graphed, whereas the graph of a non-linear relation is not a straight line. There are different ways to determine whether a relation is linear or non-linear. One way is to graph it and find out if it is a straight line or not. Linear and non-linear relations also have properties which distinguish themselves from one another, including the first differences, slopes, and degrees of the relations.

Examples

Linear Relation	Non-linear Relation
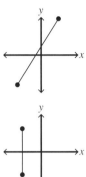	
The graph of any linear relation is a straight line.	The graph of any non-linear relation is not a straight line.

Graph the relations with the given coordinates in the table. Write the first differences in the boxes. Then fill in the blanks.

Try these!

①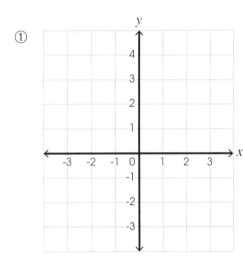

a.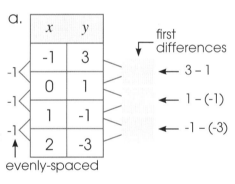

x	y	first differences
-1	3	
		← 3 – 1
0	1	
		← 1 – (-1)
1	-1	
		← -1 – (-3)
2	-3	

evenly-spaced

Hint

The first difference is the difference between two consecutive y-coordinates in which the x-coordinates are evenly-spaced.

b. Form: _____
   linear/non-linear

c. First Differences: _____
   constant/not constant

②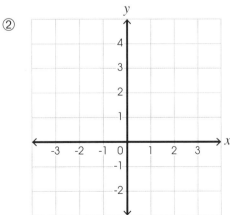

a.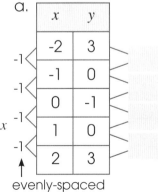

x	y
-2	3
-1	0
0	-1
1	0
2	3

← 3 – 0
← 0 – (-1)
← -1 – 0
← 0 – 3

evenly-spaced

b. Form:

_____

c. First Differences:

_____

Find the first differences with the given *x*- and *y*-values of each relation. Then graph the relations and answer the question.

③ Relation A

x	*y*
-2	0
-1	2
0	4
1	6

Relation B

x	*y*
1	-0.5
2	-1
3	-2.5
4	-5

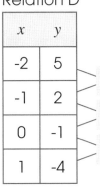

Relation C

x	*y*
-2	-5
-1	-5
0	-2
1	-2

Relation D

x	*y*
-2	5
-1	2
0	-1
1	-4

④ Describe the relationship between the shape of the relations and their first differences.

_____

_____

Find the first differences to identify whether each relation is linear or non-linear.

⑤

x	*y*
1	2
2	5
3	8
4	11

⑥

x	*y*
-8	6
-7	5.5
-6	5
-5	4.5

⑦

x	*y*
-3	15.5
-2	6
-1	2.5
0	2

Hint

If the first differences of a relation are constant, then it is linear. If a relation is non-linear, then its first differences are not constant.

_____   _____   _____

Evaluate to find the *y*-values for each relation. Determine the degree of its equation and graph it. Write whether it is linear or non-linear. Then answer the question.

⑧ $y = 2x$

x	y
-2	
-1	
0	
1	
2	

Degree:

_____

Form:

_____

⑨ $y = x^2$

x	y
-2	
-1	
0	
1	
2	

Degree:

_____

Form:

_____

Hint

The degree of a term refers to the sum of the exponents of the variables.

e.g. $2x$ ← degree: 1

x^3 ← degree: 3

x^2y ← degree: 3

⑩ $y = -x - 1$

x	y
-4	
-3	
-2	
-1	
0	

Degree:

_____

Form:

_____

⑪ $y = 0.5x^3$

x	y
-2	
-1	
0	
1	
2	

Degree:

_____

Form:

_____

⑫ $y = -\dfrac{1}{2}x + 1$

x	y
-2	
0	
2	
4	
6	

Degree:

_____

Form:

_____

Degree of Equation: 1

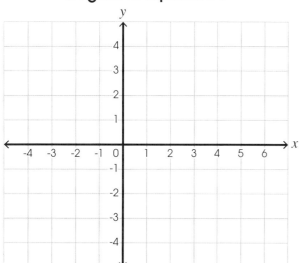

Degree of Equation: not 1

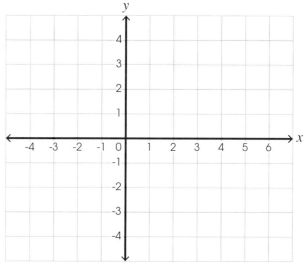

⑬   Describe the degree of the equation of each type of relation.

_____

Determine the degree of each equation to identify whether it is linear or non-linear.

⑭ $y = x^2 + 1$ _____

⑮ $y = -x$ _____

⑯ $y = 0.25x + 1$ _____

⑰ $y = x^2 + x - 1$ _____

⑱ $y = -5x + 0.4$ _____

⑲ $y = 2x^2 - x + 6$ _____

Hint

If the degree of an equation is 1, then the relation is linear. If a relation is non-linear, then the degree of its equation is not 1.

Find the slope of each pair of points. Then graph them and fill in the blanks with "constant" or "not constant".

⑳

(x,y)	m
(-2,-2)	
(-1,-1)	1
(0,0)	
(1,1)	
(2,2)	

㉑

(x,y)	m
(-2,4)	
(-1,1)	
(0,0)	
(1,1)	
(2,4)	

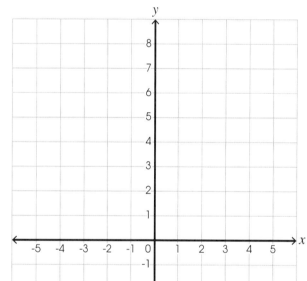

㉒

(x,y)	m
(-4,-6)	
(-2,-5.5)	
(0,-5)	
(2,-4.5)	
(4,-4)	

㉓

(x,y)	m
(-5,-3)	
(-2,-7)	
(1,-3)	
(4,-7)	
(5.5,-5)	

㉔ In a linear relation, the slopes between pairs of points are _____ .

㉕ In a non-linear relation, the slopes between pairs of points are _____ .

Complete the comparison table of linear relations and non-linear relations.

㉖

	Linear Relation	Non-linear Relation
On a Graph		
First Differences		
Degree (excluding horizontal and vertical lines)		
Slopes between Pairs of Points		

For each pair, determine which represents a linear relation and which represents a non-linear relation without graphing. Describe how you identified them.

㉗ Relation A

x	y
-2	6
-1	3
0	0
1	-3

Relation B

x	y
-4	-3
-5	0
-6	-3
-7	-12

a. Relation A: _____

   Relation B: _____

b. Explanation:

   _____

   _____

㉘ Relation C

x	y
-1	3.5
0	3
3	7.5
8	35

Relation D

x	y
-8	-1
-6	0
2	4
3	4.5

a. Relation C: _____

   Relation D: _____

b. Explanation:

   _____

   _____

㉙ a. $y = 4x + 3$

   _____

   b. $y = \dfrac{1}{2}x^2 - 1$

   _____

c. Explanation:

   _____

   _____

Answer the questions.

㉚ Consider the tables of values of the relations below.

Relation A

x	y
-2	0.4
-1	0.2
0	0
1	-0.2
2	-0.4

Relation B

x	y
-5	10
-4	7
0	-5
2	-11
3	-14

Relation C

x	y
-1	-3
0	0
1	-3
2	-12
3	-27

a. Without graphing, identify whether each relation is linear or non-linear.

b. Determining the first differences cannot be applied to Relation B to answer Question a. Explain why.

㉛ Determine whether each of the equations is linear or non-linear.

a. $y = -8 + 6x$ b. $y = -x^2 - 1$

c. $y = 2x(x + 3)$ d. $y = 4x - (3 - x)$

㉜ Karen says, "In a non-linear relation, the slope of any two sections cannot be the same because only linear relations have a constant slope." Is she correct? Explain.

㉝ Ray says, "A relation that does not have a degree of 1 must be non-linear." Is he correct? Explain.

M A T H   I R L

Both linear relations and non-linear relations are widely used to model real-life scenarios. You might already be familiar with applications of linear relations. For example, the basic relationships between speed and distance travelled, revenue and products sold, and supply and demand are all commonly modelled by linear relations. However, the applications of non-linear relations are just as important since there are many situations that are modelled by non-linear relations – one of which is an electrocardiogram (ECG). Scan this QR code to find out more about electrocardiogram and more examples of applications of non-linear relations.

Things I've learned in this chapter:

• plotting points and drawing relations on the Cartesian plane

• determining the slope of a line

• identifying the properties of a line by its slope value

• determining the x- and y-intercepts of a line

• identifying the properties of linear and non-linear relations

My Notes:

_____

_____

_____

_____

_____

_____

_____

_____

_____

_____

Chapter 1

Knowledge and Understanding

Circle the correct answers.

① A point that lies in which quadrant has negative x- and y-coordinates?

    A. Quadrant I   B. Quadrant II

    C. Quadrant III   D. Quadrant IV

② Which of the following does not represent the slope formula?

    A. $\dfrac{x_2 - x_1}{y_2 - y_1}$ B. $\dfrac{\text{change in } y}{\text{change in } x}$

    C. $\dfrac{\text{rise}}{\text{run}}$ D. $\dfrac{y_2 - y_1}{x_2 - x_1}$

③ What is the slope of a vertical line?

    A. 1   B. -1

    C. 0   D. undefined

④ Which of the following point is not a possible y-intercept?

    A. (2,0)   B. (0,5)

    C. (0,-6)   D. (0,0)

⑤ Which is not a possible number of x-intercepts for a horizontal line?

    A. none   B. exactly one

    C. infinitely many   D. none of the above

⑥ Which term refers to three points that lie on a straight line?

    A. consecutive   B. collinear

    C. constant   D. continuous

⑦ What must be constant between any pairs of points that lie on a linear relation?

    A. x-coordinates   B. y-coordinates

    C. slopes   D. all of the above

⑧ Which of the following is a non-linear relation?

    A. $y = x^2$ B. $y = x$

    C. $y = 2x$ D. $y = 3x + 5$

For each statement, write "T" for true and "F" for false.

⑨   A line with a slope that has a magnitude of 0 must be horizontal.   _____

⑩   A line that has a positive slope must be steeper than one that has a negative slope.   _____

⑪   A line that goes up from left to right must have a positive slope.   _____

⑫   A relation formed by collinear points must be linear.   _____

⑬   If $\overline{AB}$ // $\overline{CD}$, then Points A, B, C, and D must be collinear.   _____

⑭   A vertical line that passes through (3,-5) must also pass through (3,n) for any value of n.   _____

Find the slopes of each line segment with the given points. Show your work.

⑮   (-8,-3) (-2,1)   ⑯   (5,4) (7,-4)   ⑰   (-7,4) (5,-2)

Find the slopes of the lines. Show your work.

⑱

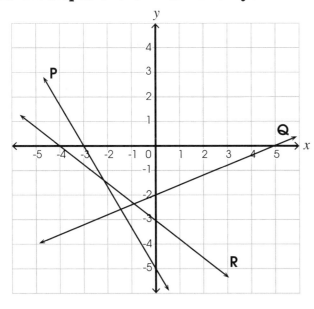

a.   Line P

b.   Line Q

c.   Line R

Determine whether the points in each set are collinear. Show your work.

⑲ A(-3,-7) B(1,1) C(4,7)

⑳ I(-2,5) J(0,-1) K(2,-6)

㉑ D(-4,0) E(0,2) F(3,3)

㉒ P(3,1) Q(-6,4) R(0,2)

Find the missing coordinates with the given information.

㉓ E(4,a) F(-2,-5) $m_{EF} = \dfrac{3}{2}$

㉔ S(-2,b) T(4,1) $m_{ST} = -\dfrac{1}{2}$

Find the slope of each line with the given description. Show your work.

㉕ a line that passes through (4,1) and has an x-intercept of 8

㉖ a line that passes through (-1,4) and has a y-intercept of -1

Find the coordinates of the *x*- and *y*-intercepts of each line that passes through each pair of points. Show your work.

㉗   (-4,-4) (2,-1)

㉘   (-6,3) (4,-2)

Match the lines with the slopes. Write the letters.

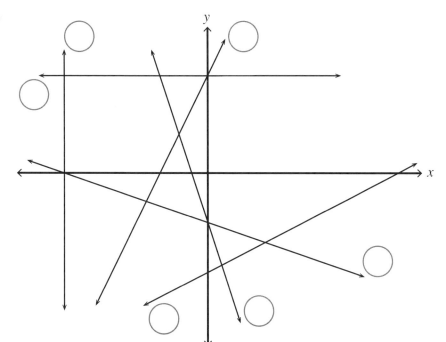

㉙

A: $m = 2$

B: $m = 0$

C: $m = -\dfrac{1}{3}$

D: $m = \text{undefined}$

E: $m = \dfrac{1}{2}$

F: $m = -3$

Application

Solve the problems. Show your work.

㉚   Kate drew two lines, $\overline{PQ}$ and $\overline{RS}$. $\overline{PQ}$ passes through (-1,5) and (1,-1); $\overline{RS}$ passes through (-4,8) and (0,-4). Determine whether the lines intersect or not without graphing.

③ Shawn drew a line to connect these points: (-4,3), (0,2), (4,-2), and (8,-3). Determine whether it is a linear or non-linear relation without graphing.

③ A line segment had endpoints at (2,5) and (7,3). Joyce extended the line segment. What is the x-intercept of the extended line?

Communication

Answer the questions.

③ Describe how you would determine whether two lines are parallel, perpendicular, or neither without graphing.

④ Consider the points (4,-5), (2,m), and (4,3). Can you determine whether they are collinear? Explain.

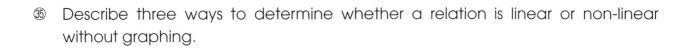

㉟ Describe three ways to determine whether a relation is linear or non-linear without graphing.

Thinking

Answer the questions.

㊱ Given that a line falls from left to right and the slope has a magnitude of $\frac{5}{2}$, if the line has a y-intercept of -2, does (-6,13) lie on the line?

㊲ The values of the x-intercept and y-intercept of a line are the same and are not 0. Determine the slope of the line algebraically.

㊳ Consider these points of a linear relation: A(x_1, y), B(x_2, y), C(x_3, y). What is the slope of the relation?

Chapter 2

Forms of Linear Equations

2.1 Slope-intercept Form: $y = mx + b$ (1)

Key Ideas

An equation of a line relates the x-coordinate and y-coordinate of any point that lies on the line. A linear equation is an equation of a straight line. It can be written in the slope-intercept form: $y = mx + b$, where m is the slope and b is the y-intercept of the line.

slope   y-intercept

$$y = mx + b$$

coordinates of any point on the line

Examples

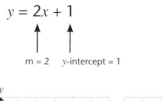

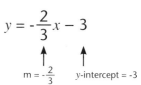

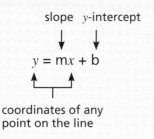

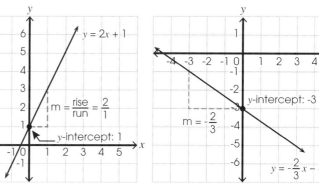

For each linear equation in the slope-intercept form, identify its slope and y-intercept. Then match it with its graph.

Try these!

① $\quad y = 2x + 3$

m = _____ y-intercept = _____

② $\quad y = \dfrac{1}{2}x + 2$

m = _____ y-intercept = _____

③ $\quad y = -3x - 1$

m = _____ y-intercept = _____

④ $\quad y = \dfrac{3}{4}x - 2$

m = _____ y-intercept = _____

A
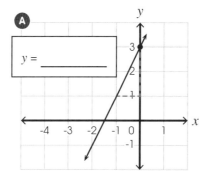
y = _____

B
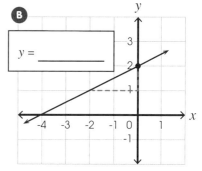
y = _____

C
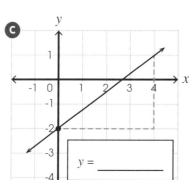
y = _____

D
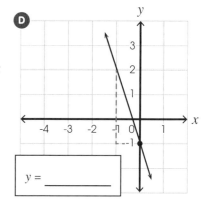
y = _____

Use the slope and *y*-intercept of each linear equation to graph it.

⑤ $y = \dfrac{1}{3}x + 2$ m = _____   *y*-intercept = _____

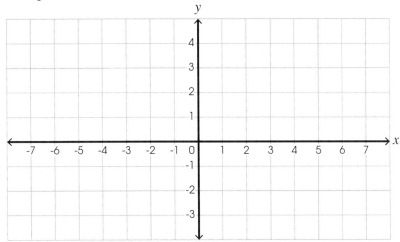

⑥ $y = \dfrac{3}{4}x - 1$ m = _____   *y*-intercept = _____

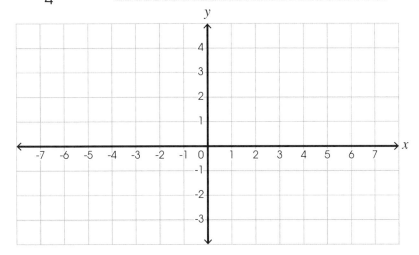

⑦ $y = -\dfrac{2}{3}x + 3$ m = _____   *y*-intercept = _____

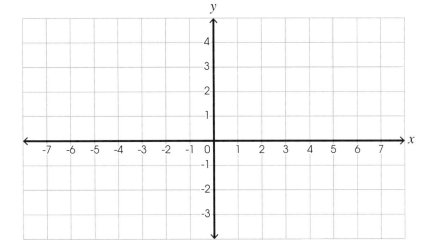

 Hint

To graph a linear equation, follow the steps below.

e.g. $y = \dfrac{2}{3}x + 1$

slope   *y*-intercept

❶ Mark the *y*-intercept.

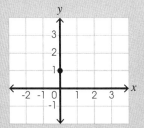

❷ Consider m = $\dfrac{\text{rise}}{\text{run}}$. If m > 0, move up from the *y*-intercept; if m < 0, move down from it.

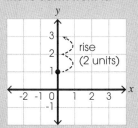

Then move to the right. Mark the point.

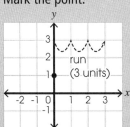

❸ Connect the *y*-intercept and the point to form a line.

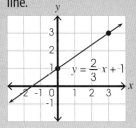

Graph the lines of the linear equations. Label the lines.

⑧ $y = 3x + 1$ (Hint: $3 = \dfrac{3}{1}$ ← rise ← run)

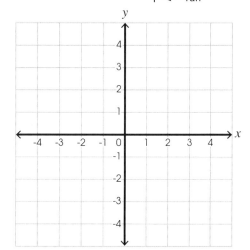

⑨ $y = -2x - 3$ (Hint: $-2 = \dfrac{-2}{1}$ ← rise ← run)

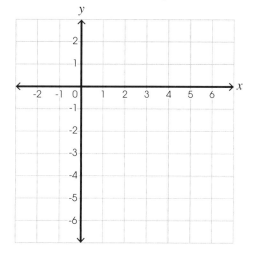

⑩ $y = 4x - 1$

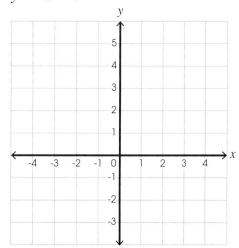

⑪ $y = -3x + 2$

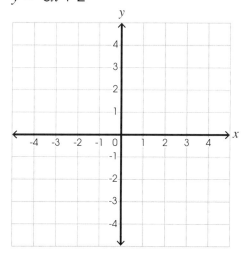

⑫

$y = \dfrac{2}{5}x - 1$

$y = -x - 2$

$y = -4x + 3$

$y = -\dfrac{3}{4}x + 1$

$y = -\dfrac{1}{3}x - 4$

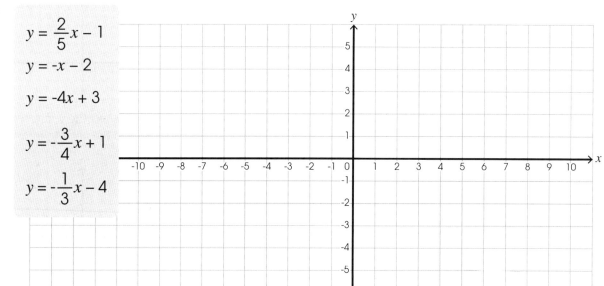

Trace the correct lines of each pair of linear equations. Label the lines.

⑬ $y = \dfrac{3}{2}x + 1$ $y = -\dfrac{2}{3}x + 1$

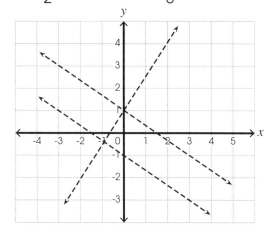

⑭ $y = -\dfrac{1}{5}x - 5$ $y = 2x - 5$

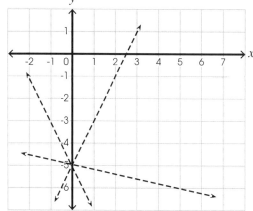

⑮ $y = \dfrac{4}{3}x + 2$ $y = \dfrac{3}{4}x + 2$

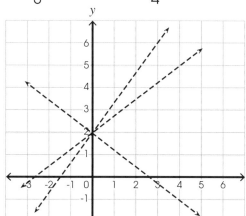

⑯ $y = -\dfrac{1}{4}x$ $y = 4x$

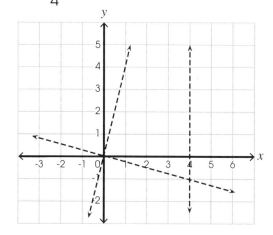

Look at the sketches of the graphs of the linear equations.
Do the matching and label the graphs.

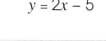

Hint

Refer to Chapter 1.3 for the properties of slopes.

⑰

$y = x - 1$ $y = -3x + 4$

$y = \dfrac{3}{2}x + 3$ $y = -x - 5$

a.
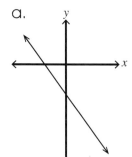

b.
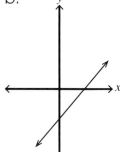

c.
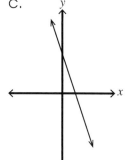

d.
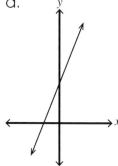

Complete the linear equation of each graph.

⑱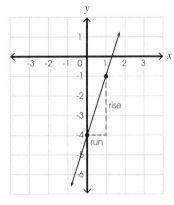

⑲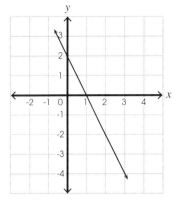

$y =$ _____

$y =$ _____

⑳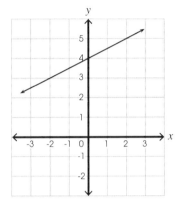

㉑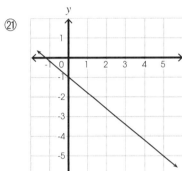

㉒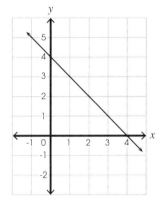

$y =$ _____

$y =$ _____

$y =$ _____

Determine the linear equations using the given points and *y*-intercepts. Show your work.

㉓ point: (2,11)
y-intercept: (0,3)

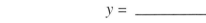

$$m = \frac{-\ 3}{-\ 0} =$$

$y =$ _____ $x +$ _____

㉔ point: (2,-1)
y-intercept: (0,2)

㉕ point: (5,-2)
y-intercept: (0,-4)

㉖ point: (8,-1)
y-intercept: (0,5)

㉗ point: (-2,4)
y-intercept: (0,-8)

_____

_____

_____

Answer the questions.

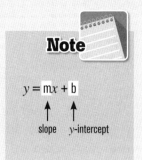

㉘ Identify the slope and y-intercept of each linear equation.

a. $y = \frac{4}{3}x + 2$ b. $y = -5x - 2$ c. $y = -x + 3$

d. $y = -4 + 6x$ e. $y = -2$ f. $y = -4x$

Note

$y = \boxed{m}x + \boxed{b}$

↑ ↑
slope y-intercept

㉙ Graph each linear equation in Question 28.

㉚ Match each linear equation with the sketch of its graph.

a. $y = -x - 2$

b. $y = -3x + 3$

c. $y = 5x - 4$

d. $y = \frac{5}{2}x + 2$

e. $y = -\frac{1}{4}x + 6$

f. $y = \frac{2}{5}x - 3$

  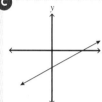
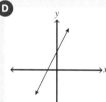 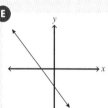 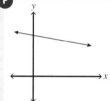

㉛ Write the linear equations of the graphs and for each pair of given points and y-intercepts.

a. 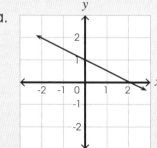 b.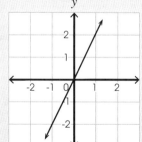

c. $(-3,1), (0,2)$

d. $(2,-12), (0,-4)$

e. $(-6,-1), (0,-3)$

f. $(-8,-9), (0,3)$

㉜ Determine whether the point $(-3,7)$ lies on the graph of $y = -x + 4$.

㉝ Describe the common property that lines in the form $y = mx$ have.

㉞ Tim says, "The line represented by $y = x + 3$ must be horizontal because x has a slope of zero." Is he correct? Explain.

㉟ Mia says, "The line represented by $y = x - 4$ can never contain a point where its x- and y-coordinates are equal." Is she correct? Explain.

Chapter 2

2.2 Slope-intercept Form: $y = mx + b$ (2)

Key Ideas

As you have learned in Chapter 2.1, we can sketch the graph of a line from the slope-intercept form of its equation, and if we are given the graph of a line, the linear equation that it represents can be determined.

In fact, a point that satisfies an equation must lie on its graph. In other words, if the x- and y-coordinates of a point satisfy an equation, then the line of the equation must pass through this point. If the coordinates do not satisfy the equation, then the point does not lie on the line.

Examples

Consider the graph of $y = 2x - 1$.

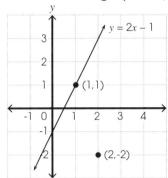

From the graph, it is obvious that $(1,1)$ lies on the line and $(2,-2)$ does not.

To determine whether a point lies on a line algebraically, substitute its x- and y-coordinates into the linear equation. If the values satisfy the equation, then it lies on the line.

- for $(1,1)$:

  $1 = 2(1) - 1$
  $1 = 2 - 1$
  $1 = 1$ ← on the line

- for $(2,-2)$:

  $-2 = 2(2) - 1$
  $-2 = 4 - 1$
  $-2 \neq 3$ ← not on the line

Determine whether the given point lies on the graph of each linear equation. Graph the line and plot the point to confirm your answer. Then fill in the blank.

Try these!

① $(4,1)$ and $y = \dfrac{1}{2}x - 1$

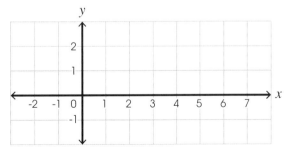

$(4,1)$ _____ on the line.
       lies/does not lie

② $(3,1)$ and $y = -\dfrac{3}{2}x + 2$

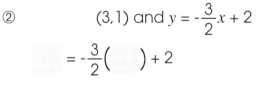

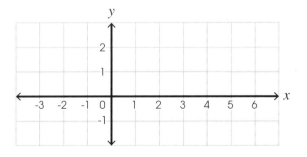

$(3,1)$ _____ on the line.

Determine whether each point lies on the graph of the linear equation. Show your work.

③ (8,-5) and $y = \dfrac{1}{2}x - 5$

④ (-4,-4) and $y = \dfrac{3}{2}x + 1$

⑤ (1,1) and $y = 5x - 4$

⑥ (-2,12) and $y = -3x + 6$

⑦ (12,-8) and $y = -\dfrac{3}{4}x + 1$

⑧ (-9,-5) and $y = -\dfrac{1}{3}x - 8$

For each point, identify the graphs of which linear equations the point lies on. Check the equations. Show your work.

⑨ (2,4)

a. $y = 6x - 8$ ◯

b. $y = \dfrac{1}{2}x + 3$ ◯

c. $y = -x + 2$ ◯

⑩ (-5,2)

a. $y = -x - 10$ ◯

b. $y = \dfrac{2}{5}x + 4$ ◯

c. $y = 2x + 12$ ◯

⑪ (4,1)

a. $y = -4x + 17$ ◯

b. $y = -\dfrac{5}{4}x + 6$ ◯

c. $y = \dfrac{3}{4}x$ ◯

Find the missing values of the points that lie on the graphs of the given linear equations. Show your work.

⑫ $y = 2x - 5$

   a. $(a, 3)$ b. $(2, b)$

Hint

Substitute the coordinates into the equation. Then solve for the unknown.

e.g. $y = 3x - 1$ and $(1, a)$

   Solve for a.
   $a = 3(1) - 1$ ← Substitute.
   $a = 2$

⑬ $y = -4x + 5$

   a. $(-2, a)$ b. $(4, b)$ c. $(c, 33)$

⑭ $y = -\dfrac{3}{5}x - 1$

   a. $(5, a)$ b. $(b, 8)$ c. $(c, 5)$

Find the coordinates of the x- and y-intercepts of each line. Show your work.

⑮ $y = 3x - 3$ ⑯ $y = -\dfrac{3}{2}x + 3$

Hint

To find the x-intercept, let $y = 0$ and solve for x.

To find the y-intercept, let $x = 0$ and solve for y.

e.g. $y = 2x + 2$

   • x-intercept:
      $0 = 2x + 2$
      $x = -1$

   • y-intercept:
      $y = 2(0) + 2$
      $y = 2$

So, the x-intercept is at $(-1, 0)$ and the y-intercept is at $(0, 2)$.

⑰ $y = -x - 2$ ⑱ $y = 2x - 6$

⑲ $y = -\dfrac{1}{4}x + 2$ ⑳ $y = -\dfrac{2}{3}x - 6$

Answer the questions.

㉑ Determine whether each point is on the graph of each linear equation.

a. (4,6) and $y = 2x - 1$

b. (-2,5) and $y = \frac{1}{2}x + 6$

c. (-6,6) and $y = -\frac{1}{3}x + 4$

d. (-2,14) and $y = -7x$

㉒ Consider the linear equations below.

- $y = 5x + 32$
- $y = \frac{5}{8}x - 2$
- $y = -\frac{3}{5}x + 4$

a. On which graph(s) does (-8,-7) lie?

b. On which graph(s) does (-5,7) lie?

c. The graphs of $y = 5x + 32$ and $y = -\frac{3}{5}x + 4$ intersect at one point. Determine this point. Explain how you know.

㉓ Determine the missing values of the points that lie on the given lines.

a. $y = -\frac{1}{2}x + 1$

- $(a,4)$
- $(4,b)$

b. $y = \frac{3}{2}x - 2$

- $(a,4)$
- $(-2,b)$

c. $y = -\frac{4}{5}x + 3$

- $(-5,a)$
- $(b,-5)$

㉔ Find the x- and y-intercepts of each line.

a. $y = -3x - 12$

b. $y = 2x$

c. $y = -\frac{1}{2}x + 1$

d. $y = -\frac{2}{3}x - 6$

㉕ Find the point on $y = -3x + 4$ where its x- and y-coordinates are the same.

Hint

㉖ Consider the linear equation $y = \frac{1}{2}x - 6$. Find the unknown values of the following points that lie on the graph.

a. (a,a)

b. $(a,-a)$

c. $(b,2b)$

d. $(3c,2c)$

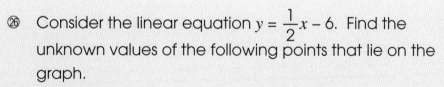

Let the point be (a,a). Then substitute them into $y = mx + b$ and solve for a.

e.g. $y = 2x - 2$

$a = 2a - 2$ ← Substitute.

$a = 2$

Point: (2,2)

㉗ Sam says, "All points that have a y-coordinate of 3 lie on the graph of $y = 3$." Is he correct? Explain.

㉘ Determine the linear equation of a line which passes through any point that has an x-coordinate of 5.

Chapter 2

2.3 Standard Form: $Ax + By + C = 0$

Key Ideas

You have learned about the slope-intercept form of linear equations. Other than in the form $y = mx + b$, a linear equation can also be written in the standard form.

Standard Form:

$Ax + By + C = 0$

or

$Ax + By = D$

where A, B, C and D are integers and $A > 0$

The slope-intercept form and the standard form are interchangeable. This means that a linear equation can be converted from one form to another to represent the same line.

Examples

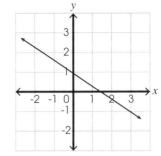

- Slope-intercept Form:
$$y = -\frac{2}{3}x + 1$$
- Standard Form:
$$2x + 3y - 3 = 0$$

If you substitute the coordinates of a point on the line (e.g. (3,-1)) into the equations, you will find that the coordinates satisfy both equations.

To convert an equation from standard form to slope-intercept form, isolate y.

$$2x + 3y - 3 = 0$$

$3y = -2x + 3$ ← isolating y

$y = -\dfrac{2}{3}x + 1$ ← slope-intercept form

Try these!

Rewrite the linear equations in slope-intercept form.

① $x + 2y - 8 = 0$

$2y = $ ____ $+$ ____ ← isolating y

$y = $ ____ $+$ ____ ← in the form of $y = mx + b$

② $3x + 2y + 10 = 0$

$2y = $ ____ $-$ ____

$y = $ ____ $-$ ____

③ $x - 2y = 10$

$-2y = $ ____

$2y = $ ____

$y = $ ____

④ $2x - 3y - 18 = 0$

$-3y = $ ____

$3y = $ ____

$= $ ____

⑤ $2x - 5y + 35 = 0$

$-5y = $ ____

$= $ ____

$= $ ____

⑥ $3x - 4y = -36$

$-4y = $ ____

$= $ ____

$= $ ____

Practice

Rewrite each linear equation in the form of $y = mx + b$. Then match it with its graph. Write the letter. Show your work.

⑦   **A** $2x + y - 4 = 0$ **B** $x - 2y + 4 = 0$

Hint

Identify the slope and y-intercept from the slope-intercept form of the linear equation to find its graph.

     C $x + 4y = -4$ **D** $x - 5y + 20 = 0$ **E** $4x - 3y = 3$

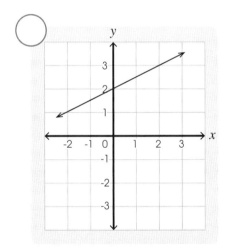

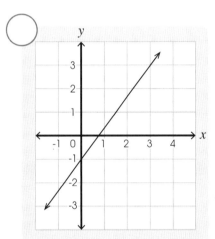

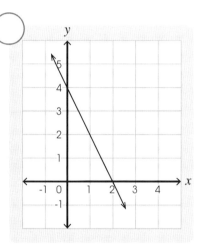

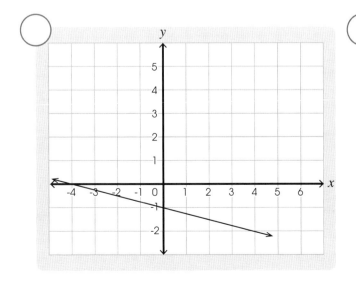

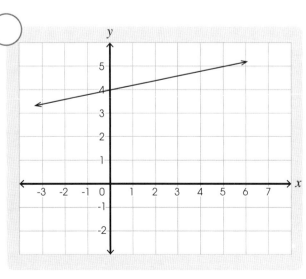

Rewrite each linear equation in the form of $y = mx + b$. Identify its slope and y-intercept. Then graph the line and label it with its standard form. Show your work.

⑧ $2x + y - 3 = 0$ ⑨ $4x - y - 1 = 0$

Hint

To graph a linear equation in standard form, rewrite it in slope-intercept form first. Then identify the slope and y-intercept to graph it.

m = _____

y-intercept = _____   m = _____

                                  y-intercept = _____

⑩ $3x + 4y = -4$ ⑪ $x - 2y + 4 = 0$ ⑫ $6x - 5y = 10$

m = _____   m = _____   m = _____

y-intercept = _____ y-intercept = _____ y-intercept = _____

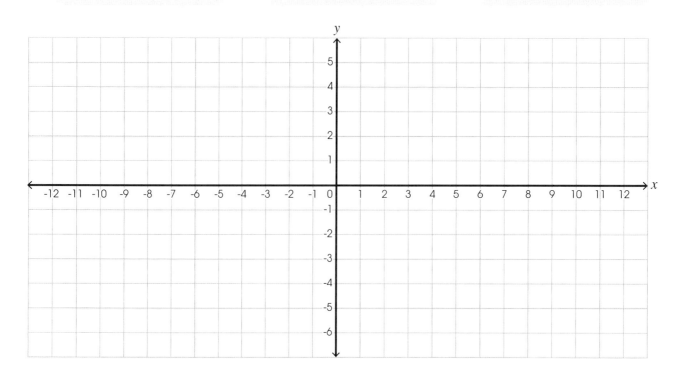

Find the *x*- and *y*-intercepts of each linear equation in standard form. Then graph it. Show your work.

⑬ $2x - y - 4 = 0$

⑭ $x - 2y + 8 = 0$

⑮ $3x - 4y = 12$

⑯ $3x + y + 3 = 0$

⑰ $2x + 3y - 12 = 0$

⑱ $x + 5y = -5$

Hint

Another way to graph a linear equation in standard form is to determine the *x*- and *y*-intercepts.

e.g. $x + y - 1 = 0$

- *x*-intercept: $(x, 0)$
$$x + 0 - 1 = 0$$
$$x = 1$$

- *y*-intercept: $(0, y)$
$$0 + y - 1 = 0$$
$$y = 1$$

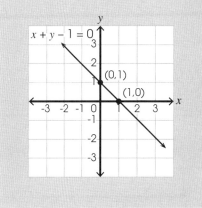

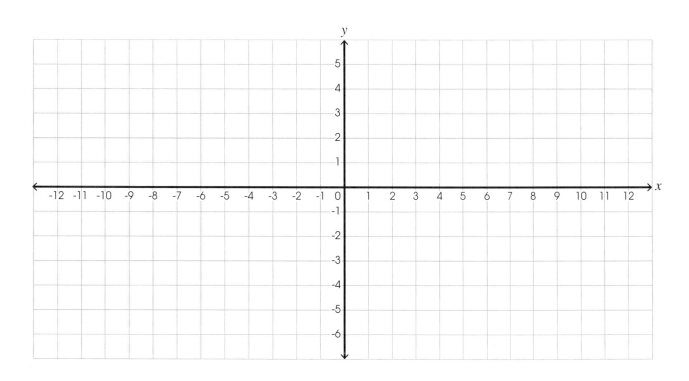

Convert each linear equation from slope-intercept form to standard form. Show your work.

⑲ $y = 5x - 1$

⑳ $y = 3x + 2$

㉑ $y = -\dfrac{1}{2}x + 6$

㉒ $y = \dfrac{3}{4}x - 4$

Hint

Move all the terms to the left side. Then multiply both sides to resolve any fractions and the negative coefficient of x, if applicable.

e.g. $y = -\dfrac{1}{2}x + 2$

$\dfrac{1}{2}x + y - 2 = 0$ ← Multiply both sides by 2.

$x + 2y - 4 = 0$ ← standard form

In $Ax + By + C = 0$, recall that A, B, and C are integers where A > 0.

㉓ $y = -\dfrac{2}{3}x + 2$

㉔ $y = -3x + 1$

㉕ $y = \dfrac{2}{5}x - 3$

Determine the linear equation of each line in standard form. Show your work.

Hint

Determine the equation in slope-intercept form first. Then convert it to standard form.

㉖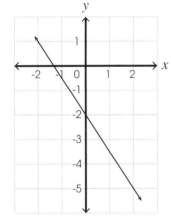

㉗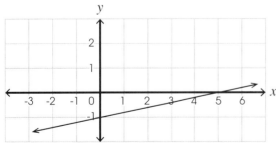

㉘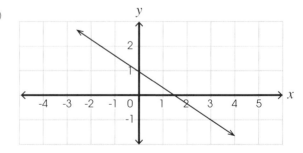

Answer the questions.

㉙ Express each linear equation in slope-intercept form.

    a. $2x + y + 1 = 0$ b. $4x - y + 2 = 0$

    c. $x + 3y = 6$ d. $x - 2y = -8$

    e. $3x - 4y + 8 = 0$ f. $2x + 3y = 9$

㉚ Express each linear equation in standard form.

    a. $y = x + 5$ b. $y = 3x - 2$

    c. $y = \dfrac{1}{2}x - 3$ d. $y = -\dfrac{3}{5}x + 2$

    e. $y = \dfrac{1}{4}x - \dfrac{3}{4}$ f. $y = -\dfrac{1}{3}x + \dfrac{2}{3}$

㉛ Determine the slope and y-intercept of each linear equation. Then graph it.

    a. $x - 2y + 2 = 0$ b. $3x + y - 5 = 0$

    c. $3x - 5y = -10$ d. $2x + 3y = 0$

㉜ Find the coordinates of the x- and y-intercepts of each linear equation. Then graph it.

    a. $5x + y - 5 = 0$ b. $x - 2y + 4 = 0$

    c. $3x + y + 6 = 0$ d. $2x - 4y - 8 = 0$

㉝ Explain how we know that $2x - y + 3 = 0$ and $y = 2x + 3$ represent the same line without graphing.

㉞ Determine whether each point lies on the line.

    a. $(1,7)$ and $3x + y - 10 = 0$ b. $(8,5)$ and $x - 2y + 2 = 0$

    c. $(-9,-3)$ and $x - 2y + 5 = 0$ d. $(3,-5)$ and $3x + 2y = -1$

    e. $(-2,-5)$ and $2y = 3x - 5$ f. $(-2,2)$ and $-3x = 10 - 2y$

㉟ Find the missing value of the point on each line.

    a. $(6,a)$ and $x + y - 3 = 0$ b. $(b,-4)$ and $2x - y + 2 = 0$

    c. $(-7,c)$ and $x - 4y = 1$ d. $(d,11)$ and $4x - 2y = 2$

    e. $(e,-5)$ and $2x + 5 = 3y$ f. $(-7,f)$ and $5y = 14 - 3x$

㊱ Determine the slope and the x- and y-intercepts of the standard form $Ax + By + C = 0$ algebraically in terms of A, B, and C.

㊲ Use your answers from Question 36 to determine the slope and x- and y-intercepts of $3x + 6y - 12 = 0$.

Chapter 2

2.4 Vertical Lines and Horizontal Lines: $x = a$, $y = b$

Key Ideas

As stated in Chapter 1, a vertical line has an undefined slope. In fact, its equation has the form $x = a$, where a is the x-intercept of the line.

A horizontal line has a slope of 0 and its equation has the form $y = b$, where b is the y-intercept.

$$y = mx + b \quad \leftarrow \text{slope-intercept form}$$
$$y = 0x + b \quad \leftarrow \text{substituting 0 for m}$$
$$y = b \quad \leftarrow \text{equation of a horizontal line}$$

Note that $x = 0$ lies on the y-axis and $y = 0$ lies on the x-axis. Any other vertical lines ($x = a$, where $a \neq 0$) do not have a y-intercept. Similarly, any other horizontal lines ($y = b$, where $b \neq 0$) do not have an x-intercept.

Examples

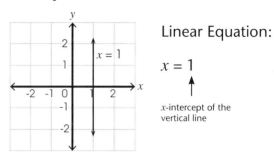

Linear Equation:

$x = 1$

↑

x-intercept of the vertical line

Consider any point on this line. Its x-coordinate must be 1 and the y-coordinate can be any value.

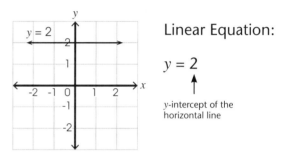

Linear Equation:

$y = 2$

↑

y-intercept of the horizontal line

Consider any point on this line. Its x-coordinate can be any value and the y-coordinate must be 2.

Write the linear equations of the vertical and horizontal lines.

Try these!

①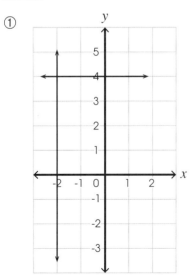

$x =$ ⬜ ← x-intercept of vertical line

$y =$ ⬜ ← y-intercept of horizontal line

②

$x =$ ⬜ ← x-intercept

$y =$ ⬜ ← y-intercept

③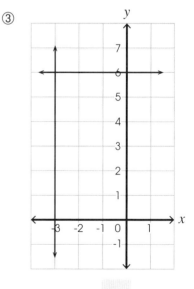

$x =$ ⬜

$y =$ ⬜

Graph each line. Circle "vertical" or "horizontal" to describe each line and write the coordinates of two points that lie on the line. Then answer the questions.

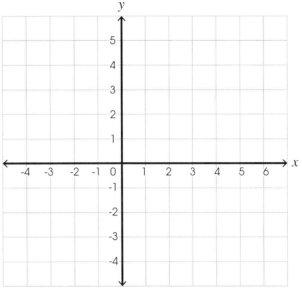

④ $x = -1$

• Line: vertical / horizontal

• Points: _____ , _____

⑤ $y = 3$

• Line: vertical / horizontal

• Points: _____ , _____

⑥ $x = 5$

• Line: vertical / horizontal

• Points: _____ , _____

⑦ $y = -4$

• Line: vertical / horizontal

• Points: _____ , _____

⑧ The point (-2,-4) lies on $y = -4$. If this graph were not given, could you determine whether this point lies on this line? If so, how?

_____

_____

Match each equation with its graph. Write the letter.

⑨   Ⓐ $y = -3$

Ⓑ $x = -4$

Ⓒ $y = 3$

Ⓓ $x = 4$

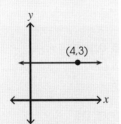
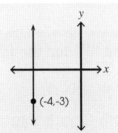
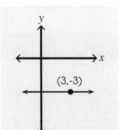
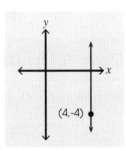

_____   _____   _____   _____

Each point passes through a vertical line and a horizontal line. Write the equations of these lines in the table.

⑩

	(1,3)	(2,-6)	(-4,3)	(5,-2)	(7,0)
Vertical Line					
Horizontal Line					

Match the point with the line(s) that it lies on.

⑪ (-3,1) •

(2,-1) •

(-1,3) •

(2,3) •

• $x = 2$

• $x = -1$

• $y = 1$

• $y = 3$

⑫ (-1,3) •

(1,5) •

(-1,-3) •

(2,-3) •

• $x = -1$

• $x = 2$

• $y = -3$

• $y = 5$

Match each equation with the description of its graph.

⑬ $x = -1$ $x = 2$ $x = 3$ $y = -2$ $y = 1$ $y = -4$

a. a horizontal line that passes through (-4,-2)   _____

b. a line that passes through (-1,1) and has a y-intercept only   _____

c. a line that has an x-intercept of 2 and no y-intercept   _____

d. a vertical line that passes through (3,1)   _____

e. a line that passes through (-1,-4) and has an x-intercept only   _____

f. a line that has a y-intercept of -4 and no x-intercept   _____

Circle "T" for the true statements and "F" for the false ones.

⑭ All vertical lines have an undefined slope.   T / F

⑮ A horizontal line cannot lie in both Quadrants II and III.   T / F

⑯ A vertical line must have one y-intercept.   T / F

⑰ The graph of $x = 0$ lies on the x-axis.   T / F

⑱ All the points on a vertical line have the same x-coordinate.   T / F

⑲ All horizontal lines pass through (0,0).   T / F

⑳ A horizontal line has either no x-intercept or infinitely many x-intercepts.   T / F

㉑ Consider the graphs of $x = a$ and $y = b$. The point where they intersect must have the coordinates of (a,b).   T / F

Answer the questions.

㉒ Write the equations of the vertical and horizontal lines.

a.

y

• (3,4)

→ x

b.

y

← → x

(-2,-5) •

c.

y

← → x

• (2,-3)

d.

y

← → x

• (-5,-3)

㉓ Determine the coordinates of the intercept of each line.

a. $x = -6$ b. $y = -2$ c. $x = -9$

d. $x = 15$ e. $y = 7$ f. $y = -8$

㉔ Determine which quadrants each line lies in.

a. $y = -4$ b. $x = 5$ c. $y = 10$

d. $x = -1$ e. $y = 3$ f. $x = 3$

㉕ Linda says, "There is not enough information to determine the value of a in the point $(a,5)$ that lies on $x = 2$." Is she correct? Explain.

㉖ Determine the point that lies on both lines.

a. $x = 3$ and $y = -1$ b. $x = -2$ and $y = 4$

c. $x = -3$ and $y = -2$ d. $x = 11$ and $y = -8$

㉗ Each given point below is the intersection of a vertical line and a horizontal line. Determine the equations of the lines for each point.

a. (2,9) b. (-4,3) c. (7,-5)

d. (-3,-4) e. (6,-1) f. (0,-3)

㉘ Determine the equations of the vertical and horizontal lines that do not lie in any quadrants.

Hint

㉙ Show the steps to derive the equation of a horizontal line from $y = mx + b$.

The slope of a horizontal line is 0.

㉚ The points (4,7), (4,3), (-2,7), and (-2,3) are the vertices of a rectangle. Write an equation for the line that makes up each side of the rectangle.

㉛ The point (-2,4) is the corner of a square and two of its sides are represented by $x = 5$ and $y = -3$. Find the other points of the square and the equations of the remaining sides.

㉜ Explain why a point cannot lie on more than one horizontal line.

Chapter 2

2.5   Equation of a Line

Key Ideas

In Chapter 2.1, you have learned to determine the linear equation of a line using the y-intercept and a point on the line.

❶ Find the slope by substituting the given values into $y = mx + b$ and solving for m.

❷ Using the slope and the given y-intercept to write the equation.

If you are given the slope of a line and a point, you can use a similar method to determine the equation.

❶ Find the y-intercept by substituting the given values into $y = mx + b$ and solving for b.

❷ Use the y-intercept and the given slope to write the equation.

Examples

Given: y-intercept and one point

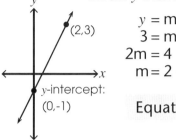

$$y = mx + b$$
$$3 = m(2) + (-1) \leftarrow \text{substituting}$$
$$2m = 4$$
$$m = 2 \leftarrow \text{slope}$$

Equation: $y = 2x - 1$
↑ slope   ↑ y-intercept (given)

Given: slope and one point

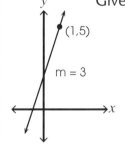

$$y = mx + b$$
$$5 = (3)(1) + b \leftarrow \text{substituting}$$
$$b = 5 - 3$$
$$b = 2 \leftarrow y\text{-intercept}$$

Equation: $y = 3x + 2$
↑ slope   ↑ y-intercept (given)

Try these!

Find the equations of the lines with the given information.

① Given: y-intercept, one point

a line that has a y-intercept of 3 and passes through (1,5)

$\boxed{} = m(\boxed{}) + \boxed{}$ ← Substitute the known values and solve for m.

m = _____ y-intercept: _____

Equation: $y =$ _____ $x +$ _____

② Given: slope, one point

a line that has a slope of -3 and passes through (-1,4)

$\boxed{} = (\boxed{})(\boxed{}) + b$ ← Substitute the known values and solve for b.

m = _____ y-intercept: _____

Equation: $y =$ _____ $x +$ _____

Find the linear equations in slope-intercept form with the given information. Show your work.

③ a. passes through (-3,-1) and has a
    y-intercept of 5

    b. passes through (-1,3) and has a
    y-intercept of -1

    c. passes through (4,-5) and has a
    y-intercept of -8

    d. passes through (5,1) and has a
    y-intercept of -3

    e. passes through (16,0) and has a
    y-intercept of 8

④ a. passes through (3,3) and has a
    slope of 2

    b. passes through (-1,-6) and has a
    slope of 5

    c. passes through (12,-3) and has a
    slope of -1

    d. passes through (4,-7) and has a
    slope of $-\frac{5}{2}$

    e. passes through (-3,7) and has a
    slope of $-\frac{4}{3}$

Find the equation of each line in slope-intercept form with the two given points. Show your work.

⑤ (3,1) (-1,9)

- slope:

$$m = \dfrac{ - }{ - } =$$

- y-intercept:

$$ = ()() + b$$

$$=$$

$$y = \underline{}$$

⑥ (-1,-1) (2,11)

- slope:

- y-intercept:

$$y = \underline{}$$

Hint

If you are given two points on a line, its equation can be determined.

e.g. a line that passes through (1,-2) and (3,4)

❶ Find the slope using the slope formula.

$$m = \dfrac{4 - (-2)}{3 - 1} = 3$$

❷ Find the y-intercept using the slope and one of the points.

$$-2 = (3)(1) + b$$

$$b = -5$$

Equation: $y = 3x - 5$

⑦ (8,1) (-4,-2)

⑧ (-3,-4) (6,2)

⑨ (-4,-1) (-6,-4)

⑩ (-5,-6) (5,-10)

⑪ (-2,7) (-4,8)

⑫ (0,-2) (5,2)

Find the equations of the lines in standard form with the given information. Show your work.

⑬ (1,11) and a *y*-intercept of 9

⑭ (-1,2) and a slope of -8

Hint

To convert an equation from slope-intercept form to standard form, rearrange the terms.

Standard Form*

$$Ax + By + C = 0$$

or

$$Ax + By = D$$

where A, B, C, and D are integers and A > 0

*Refer to Chapter 2.3 to revisit the concepts on standard form of equations.

⑮ (6,2) and (-3,-4)

⑯ (-3,9) and a *y*-intercept of 5

⑰ (3,-5) and a slope of -4

⑱ (4,-7) and a slope of $-\frac{5}{2}$

⑲ (-4,3) and (-10,-3)

⑳ an *x*-intercept of -20 and a *y*-intercept of -10

㉑ an *x*-intercept of -6 and a slope of $\frac{1}{2}$

㉒ (-9,-4) and an *x*-intercept of -3

Find the unknowns. Show your work.

㉓ What is the y-intercept, b, in the equation $y = 2x + b$ if it passes through

    a. (2,8)?   b. (7,8)?   c. (-3,4)?

㉔ What is the slope, m, in the equation $y = mx - 5$ if it passes through

    a. (3,7)?   b. (-4,7)?   c. (-3,-3)?

㉕ What is the value of A in the equation $Ax + y - 2 = 0$ if it passes through

    a. (-1,5)?   b. (2,-12)?   c. (5,-18)?

㉖ What is the value of B in the equation $x + By + 1 = 0$ if it passes through

    a. (-7,2)?   b. (7,4)?   c. (11,2)?

㉗ What is the value of C in the equation $2x - y + C = 0$ if it passes through

    a. (-1,1)?   b. (3,1)?   c. (-3,2)?

㉘ What is the value of D in the equation $3x - 2y = D$ if it passes through

    a. (2,6)?   b. (-2,-5)?   c. (-5,-3)?

Answer the questions.

㉙ Find the equation in slope-intercept form of each line that passes through the given points.

   a. (-1,-4) and (3,8)   b. (-4,1) and (6,6)

   c. (-2,12) and (5,-2)   d. (-8,3) and (-4,-3)

㉚ Find the standard form of each line that has the given slope and passes through the given point.

   a. slope $= -\frac{1}{3}$ and (5,1)   b. slope $= 2$ and (2,6)

   c. slope $= \frac{3}{2}$ and (-3,-5)   d. slope $= -\frac{1}{4}$ and (7,-3)

㉛ Determine the unknown value in bold for each equation if it passes through (-4,3).

   a. $y = \mathbf{m}x + 4$ b. $y = -2x + \mathbf{b}$

   c. $\mathbf{A}x - y + 2 = 0$ d. $3x + \mathbf{B}y - 6 = 0$

Note

The equation of a vertical line is $x = a$. It has an undefined slope. The equation of a horizontal line is $y = b$. It has a slope of 0.

㉜ Consider these points: A(6,12), B(-4,-3), C(-2,6), and D(-4,6). Find the equations of the line segments.

   a. $\overline{AB}$ b. $\overline{BC}$

   c. $\overline{BD}$ d. $\overline{CD}$

㉝ Is the following information enough to determine the equation of a line?

   a. a point the line passes through and the x-intercept
   b. the value of A in the standard form and the y-intercept
   c. the y-intercept and the magnitude of the slope

㉞ Find the equations that represent the sides of the triangle formed by the points (4,-5), (1,1), and (-3,-5).

㉟ Determine the equation of the line that has the same slope as $y = -2x + 3$ and the same y-intercept as $y = 3x - 2$.

㊱ Determine the equation of the line that has the same x-intercept as $x + 2y + 4 = 0$ and the same y-intercept as $3x - y + 2 = 0$.

㊲ The points (-1,6), (5,6), (3,2), and (-3,2) form a parallelogram.

   a. Find the equations of its sides.
   b. Find the equations of its diagonals.

Hint

Make a sketch of the parallelogram to identify its sides and diagonals.

Chapter 2

2.6 Relating Linear Equations

Key Ideas

The relationship between the graphs of two linear equations can be determined by their slopes.

Consider that the slopes of two linear equations are the same. If their y-intercepts are also the same, then they are equivalent linear equations and represent the same line. If their y-intercepts are different, then the lines are parallel.

If the slopes of the two linear equations are different, then they must intersect at one point. In fact, if their slopes are negative reciprocals of each other, then the lines are perpendicular (intersecting at 90°).

Examples

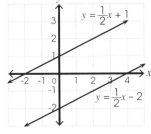

Consider the graphs of
$y = \frac{1}{2}x + 1$ and $y = \frac{1}{2}x - 2$.
• same slope of $\frac{1}{2}$
• different y-intercepts
The lines are parallel.

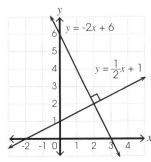

Consider the graphs of
$y = \frac{1}{2}x + 1$ and $y = -2x + 6$.
• different slopes
• slopes are negative reciprocals
The lines are perpendicular.

Try these!

Graph the lines. Then fill in the blanks.

① **same slope**

$y = 2x + 1$ $y = 2x - 3$ $2x - y + 1 = 0$

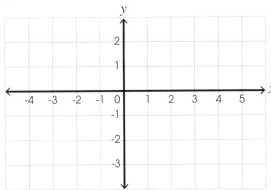

a. $y = 2x + 1$ and $y = 2x - 3$

• same slope ← slope = 2

• _____ y-intercept(s)

They are _____ .
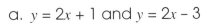
$\qquad$ parallel/equivalent

b. $y = 2x + 1$ and $2x - y + 1 = 0$

• same slope

• _____ y-intercept(s)

They are _____ .

② **different slopes**

$y = \frac{1}{3}x$ $y = -3x$ $y = \frac{2}{3}x - 1$

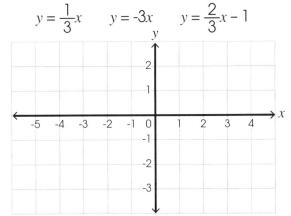

a. $y = \frac{1}{3}x$ and $y = -3x$

• slopes: different and _____
  negative reciprocals   are/are not

They intersect and _____
perpendicular.   are/are not

b. $y = \frac{1}{3}x$ and $y = \frac{2}{3}x - 1$

• slopes: different and _____
  negative reciprocals

They intersect and _____
perpendicular.

Compare the slopes and *y*-intercepts of the lines in each pair to identify whether they are parallel or equivalent. Circle the words and fill in the blank. Then graph them to check your answers.

③
$$y = x + 1$$
$$x - y + 1 = 0$$ ← Convert to slope-intercept form.

④
$$y = -2x + 3$$
$$2x + y + 2 = 0$$

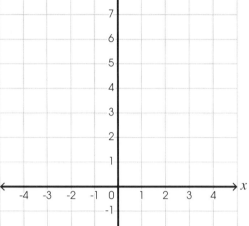

③
- slopes:
  same / different

- *y*-intercepts:
  same / different

_____
parallel/equivalent

④
- slopes:
  same / different

- *y*-intercepts:
  same / different

_____

⑤
$$y = \frac{1}{3}x + 3$$
$$x - 3y - 6 = 0$$

⑥
$$3x + 4y = -16$$
$$y = -\frac{3}{4}x - 4$$

⑤
- slopes:
  same / different

- *y*-intercepts:
  same / different

_____

⑥
- slopes:
  same / different

- *y*-intercepts:
  same / different

_____

Determine whether the lines in each pair have slopes that are negative reciprocals of each other to identify whether they are perpendicular. Circle the word(s) and fill in the blank. Then graph them to check your answers.

⑦
$$y = 4x - 2 \qquad y = -\frac{1}{4}x + 1$$

slopes: are / are not   negative reciprocals

_____
perpendicular/not perpendicular

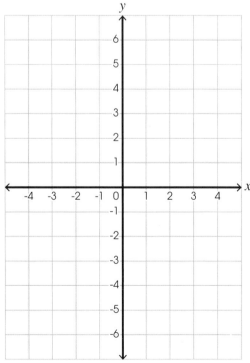

⑧
$$y = x + 5 \qquad x + y - 3 = 0$$

slopes: are / are not   negative reciprocals

_____

⑨
$$y = 2x - 3 \qquad x - 2y = -4$$

slopes: are / are not   negative reciprocals

_____

Determine whether the linear equations in each pair are equivalent algebraically. Show your work.

⑩ $y = -x - 1$

   $x + y - 1 = 0$

⑪ $y = -\dfrac{1}{2}x - 4$

   $x + 2y + 8 = 0$

⑫ $y = \dfrac{3}{5}x + 2$

   $3x - 5y + 10 = 0$

⑬ $y = 2x + 3$

   $2x + y = -3$

⑭ $2x + 2y + 2 = 0$

   $4x + 2y = -4$

⑮ $3x + 2y = -4$

   $2x - 3y = 6$

For each pair of equations, determine whether their lines are equivalent, parallel, or perpendicular algebraically.

⑯ $x - 4y = 4$

   $y = -4x + 1$

⑰ $2x - y + 3 = 0$

   $4x - 2y = 6$

⑱ $y = -\dfrac{1}{2}x + 2$

   $x + 2y = 4$

⑲ $y = -5x + 3$

   $5x + y = 3$

⑳ $y = 2x + 6$

   $x + 2y - 12 = 0$

㉑ $y = \dfrac{1}{4}x + 5$

   $x - 4y - 20 = 0$

Answer the questions.

㉒ Which lines are equivalent to $4x - 2y = -8$?

   a. $y = 2x + 4$ b. $2x - y + 4 = 0$

   c. $6x - 3y + 12 = 0$ d. $y = 2x - 4$

㉓ Which lines are parallel to $y = \frac{1}{2}x - 1$?

   a. $y = \frac{1}{2}x + 5$ b. $x + 2y = 0$

   c. $x - 2y + 8 = 0$ d. $x - 2y = 4$

㉔ Which lines are perpendicular to $y = -5x + 2$?

   a. $y = -\frac{1}{5}x - 2$ b. $y = \frac{1}{5}x + 4$

   c. $5x + y - 8 = 0$ d. $x - 5y = -9$

㉕ Determine whether the lines in each pair are equivalent, parallel, or perpendicular.

   a. $y = -3x + 1$ b. $y = -\frac{3}{2}x + 3$

       $6x + 2y - 2 = 0$ $3x + 2y = -12$

   c. $4x + 3y = 6$ d. $3x - 5y = 5$

       $8x + 6y + 9 = 0$ $5x + 3y + 6 = 0$

㉖ Consider the linear equation $2x - 7y + 14 = 0$.

   a. Write an equation that is parallel to it and has a y-intercept of -4.

   b. Write an equation that is perpendicular to it and has a y-intercept of 8.

㉗ If the linear equations in a set have the same x-intercept, describe a condition in which their slopes must satisfy for the lines to be equivalent.

㉘ The linear equations $y = \frac{1}{2}x + 2$ and $Ax - 4y = -8$ are equivalent. Find the value of A.

Hint

Substitute the value of y of the first equation into the second equation.

㉙ The linear equations $4x + y - 2 = 0$ and $2x - By - 12 = 0$ are perpendicular. Find the value of B.

Things I have learned in this chapter:

• identifying the slope and y-intercept from a linear equation

• graphing the lines of linear equations

• determining the equation of a line in slope-intercept form and standard form

• understanding the properties of equivalent, parallel, and perpendicular lines

Notes:

_____

_____

_____

_____

_____

_____

_____

_____

_____

Chapter 2

Knowledge and Understanding

Circle the correct answers.

① Which is the slope-intercept form?

    A. $Ax + By = D$ B. $y = mx + b$

    C. $Ax + By + C = 0$ D. $x = a, y = b$

② Which line has a y-intercept of -2?

    A. $y = -2x + 1$ B. $y = x + 2$

    C. $y = -2x + 2$ D. $y = 5x - 2$

③ Which line has a positive slope?

    A. $2x + y = 8$ B. $x + 2y + 1 = 0$

    C. $y = -\dfrac{2}{3}x + 5$ D. $2x = y + 5$

④ Which represents a horizontal line?

    A. $y = -4$ B. $x = 2$

    C. $y = -3x$ D. $y = x$

⑤ Which line does not have a y-intercept?

    A. $y = -1$ B. $x = 3$

    C. $y = 5$ D. $x = y$

⑥ Which line does not pass through the origin?

    A. $y = 0$ B. $y = -x$

    C. $x = 0$ D. $x + y = 1$

⑦ Which equation is not equivalent to the rest?

    A. $3x + y - 6 = 0$ B. $y = -\dfrac{1}{3}x + 2$

    C. $x + 3y = 6$ D. $2x + 6y = 12$

⑧ What is the slope of a line that is parallel to $y = 4x - 7$?

    A. -4   B. $\dfrac{1}{4}$

    C. $-\dfrac{1}{4}$ D. 4

Graph the lines and label them.

⑨　$y = 3x - 4$　　　　　　$y = -\dfrac{1}{2}x + 2$　　　　　$y = \dfrac{2}{3}x$　　　　　$y = -\dfrac{3}{2}x - 3$

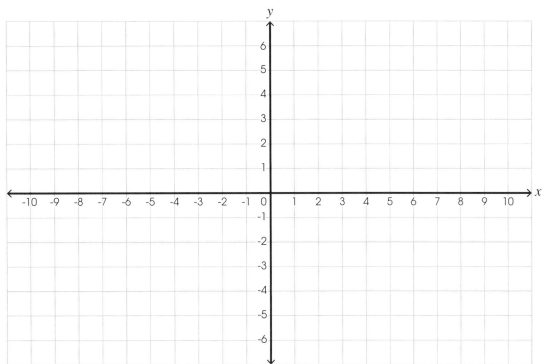

Find the slope of the line that passes through each pair of points. Show your work.

⑩　(-2,11)　(2,-1)　　　　⑪　(0,-5)　(-6,-6)　　　　⑫　(2,5)　(2,-2)

⑬　(-3,-5)　(3,-5)　　　　⑭　(5,1)　(-5,-3)　　　　⑮　(-3,4)　(3,-4)

Convert each linear equation from standard form to slope-intercept form. Then identify its slope and y-intercept.

⑯　$3x + y - 5 = 0$　　　　⑰　$2x - 3y + 9 = 0$　　　　⑱　$x + 6y = 30$

Determine whether each point lies on the line. Show your work.

⑲ $y = \dfrac{2}{3}x + 6$ and $(6,6)$ ⑳ $y = -\dfrac{1}{4}x - 4$ and $(-7,-2)$ ㉑ $3x - 2y = -4$ and $(-2,-1)$

Find the equations of the lines with the given information. Write the equations in slope-intercept form and standard form.

㉒ a slope of $-\dfrac{3}{2}$ and a y-intercept of -3

㉓ an x-intercept of -4 and a y-intercept of 2

㉔ passes through $(4,2)$ and $(1,-4)$

㉕ passes through $(-8,-1)$ and $(2,-6)$

㉖ passes through $(-2,-4)$ and $(2,-1)$

㉗ passes through $(-1,2)$ and $(-2,-3)$

Describe how the graphs of the linear equations in each pair are related.

㉘ $2x - 2y = 8$

$y = x - 4$

_____

㉙ $x - 5y = 10$

$y = \dfrac{1}{5}x + 1$

_____

㉚ $y = \dfrac{3}{5}x + 2$

$3x - 5y = -10$

_____

㉛ $3x + 9y + 2 = 0$

$y = 3x - 7$

_____

㉜ $y = -\dfrac{1}{3}x + 6$

$x + 3y - 15 = 0$

_____

㉝ $y = -7x + 4$

$-x + 7y - 7 = 0$

_____

Find the values of h. Show your work.

㉞ (-4,h) on $y = 2x + 5$

㉟ (h,-2) on $2x + 3y - 2 = 0$

㊱ $y = hx + 4$ passes through (6,7)

㊲ $2x - y + h = 0$ passes through (1,-2)

㊳ $2x - hy = 6$ passes through (-6,-2)

㊴ $hx - 3y + 9 = 0$ passes through (-3,8)

Application

Solve the problems. Show your work.

㊵ Natalie drew a line that passes through (5,-1) and intersects with the y-axis at (0,3). Find the equation of the line in slope-intercept form.

㊶ Adrian wants to draw a line that passes through (6,5) and lies in Quadrant I and Quadrant III only. Is it possible? If so, find the equation of the line in slope-intercept form.

㊷ A vertical line and a horizontal line are drawn. If they intersect at (2,-3), what are the equations of the lines?

㊸ Ron graphed the lines of two linear equations and realized that they are the same line. Which of the linear equations did he graph: $4x + y - 3 = 0$, $y = -4x + 3$, and $4x + y = -3$?

Communication

Answer the questions.

㊹ Describe one benefit of representing linear equations in slope-intercept form over standard form, and vice versa.

㊺ Describe how to determine whether two lines are perpendicular.

㊻ Describe the steps required to find the equation of a line if two points that lie on it are given.

Thinking

Find the coordinates of the points. Show your work.

(47) $(a, -2a)$ lies on $y = -\frac{1}{2}x + 3$

(48) $(a, \frac{1}{4}a)$ lies on $x - 5y + 3 = 0$

Find the point on each line where its *x*- and *y*-coordinates are the same. Show your work.

(49) $x + y - 4 = 0$

(50) $x - 2y + 4 = 0$

Answer the questions. Show your work.

(51) Determine the equation of the line that has the same slope as $3x - 4y - 4 = 0$ and the same y-intercept as $x + 2y = -4$.

(52) Determine the equation of the line that has the same x-intercept as $y = -\frac{1}{2}x - 2$ and the same y-intercept as $x - 2y + 16 = 0$.

(53) If the points (3,1) and (-1,1) form one side of a square, write all the possible equations for the sides of the square.

(54) Determine the value of B so that $y = -\frac{2}{3}x + 6$ and $2x + By - 18 = 0$ are equivalent equations.

Interpreting Linear Equations

3.1   Points of Intersection

Key Ideas

The graphs of two linear equations can have any one of the following:

- one point of intersection or
- no points of intersection (the graphs are parallel) or
- infinite points of intersection (the equations are equivalent)

Any point of intersection of two linear equations must lie on both graphs and must satisfy both equations.

Examples

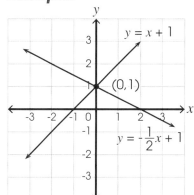

The point of intersection of the linear equations is (0,1).

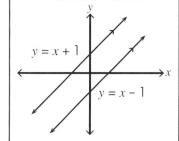

Parallel Lines

no points of intersection

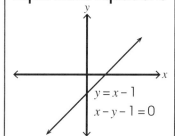

Equivalent Equations

infinite points of intersection

Indicate the point of intersection for each pair of lines. Write its coordinates.

Try these!

①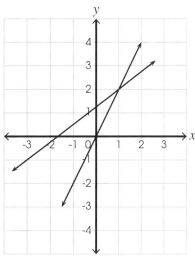

Point of Intersection:

(___ , ___)

②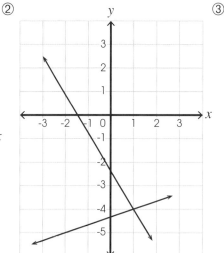

Point of Intersection:

(___ , ___)

③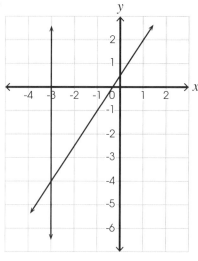

Point of Intersection:

(___ , ___)

Determine the points of intersection of the lines.

④

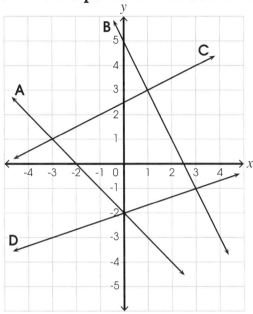

Points of Intersection:

a. Lines A and C: _____

b. Lines B and D: _____

c. Lines A and D: _____

d. Lines B and C: _____

⑤

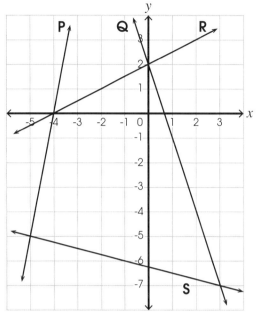

Points of Intersection:

a. Lines P and R: _____

b. Lines P and S: _____

c. Lines Q and R: _____

d. Lines Q and S: _____

Graph the linear equations. Then determine the points of intersection.

⑥ $y = -\dfrac{1}{3}x + 1$

$y = -2x - 4$

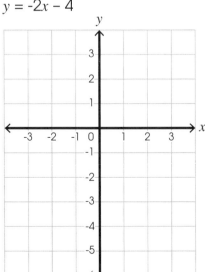

_____

⑦ $y = \dfrac{1}{2}x - 2$

$y = 3x + 3$

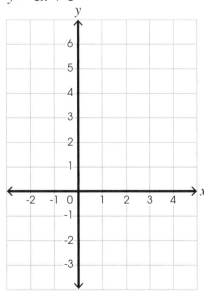

_____

⑧ $y = -4x + 1$

$x = 1$

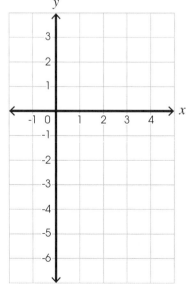

_____

Analytic Geometry (**Grade 9**)   **75**

Graph the linear equations and determine the points of intersection. Answer the questions.

⑨

Line A: $x - 3y - 8 = 0$

Line B: $y = -\dfrac{1}{2}x + 4$

Line C: $x + 2y - 8 = 0$

Line D: $2x - y + 4 = 0$

Line E: $y = 2x - 1$

Line F: $y = -3x - 6$

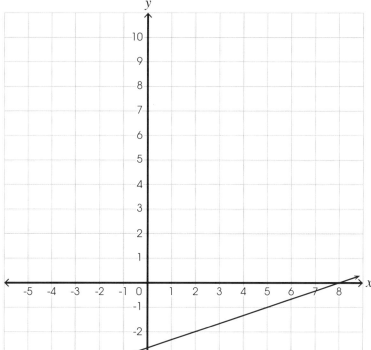

a. Lines A and B: _____

b. Lines A and D: _____

c. Lines A and E: _____

d. Lines C and D: _____

e. Lines C and E: _____

f. Lines C and F: _____

⑩ Do Lines D and E intersect? If they do, how many points of intersection do they have? How do you know?

_____

⑪ Do Lines B and C intersect? If they do, how many points of intersection do they have? How do you know?

_____

⑫ How many lines intersect at (-1,-3)? Name the lines that intersect at this point.

_____

Determine whether each point is a point of intersection of each pair of lines.

⑬   (0,-2)

$y = 2x - 2$

$y = -\dfrac{1}{2}x - 2$

⑭   (-4,4)

$y = -\dfrac{1}{2}x + 2$

$3x + 4y + 3 = 0$

Hint

Substitute the coordinates into each equation. If the coordinates satisfy both equations, then the point is a point of intersection.

For the linear equations in each pair, determine whether they are parallel, equivalent, or intersect at one point. Check the correct circle. If they intersect at one point, circle the point of intersection.

⑮ $y = 2x + 1$

$y = -x + 4$

○ parallel

○ equivalent

○ intersect at one point:
   (1,3) / (3,1)

⑯ $y = \dfrac{3}{5}x + 1$

$y = \dfrac{3}{5}x - 5$

○ parallel

○ equivalent

○ intersect at one point:
   (-5,-2) / (5,-2)

Hint

Determine the slopes and y-intercepts of the lines.

• parallel lines:
  same slope, different y-intercepts

• equivalent lines:
  same slope, same y-intercept

• intersect at one point:
  different slopes, y-intercepts may or may not be the same

⑰ $y = \dfrac{1}{2}x - 2$

$x + 2y = 0$

○ parallel

○ equivalent

○ intersect at one point:
   (-2,1) / (2,-1)

⑱ $y = \dfrac{5}{2}x + 4$

$5x - 2y = -8$

○ parallel

○ equivalent

○ intersect at one point:
   (0,4) / (-4,-6)

⑲ $4x - 3y - 18 = 0$

$y = \dfrac{4}{3}x + 1$

○ parallel

○ equivalent

○ intersect at one point:
   (3,-2) / (-3,-3)

⑳ $2x - 3y = -15$

$x + 3y + 3 = 0$

○ parallel

○ equivalent

○ intersect at one point:
   (-6,1) / (-3,0)

Graph the lines to solve the equations. Then check your answers by substitution.

㉑ $2x - y = -3$ $x + y = -3$

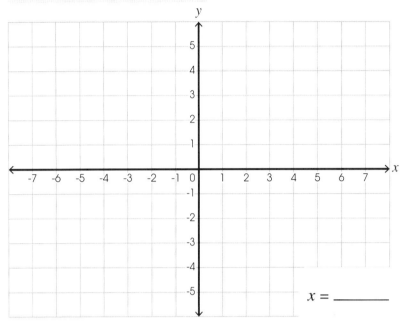

$x =$ _____

$y =$ _____

Check:

Hint

The point of intersection represents the solution that solves the linear equations.

e.g. Solve for x and y.

$$2x - y - 1 = 0$$
$$-x - y = -5$$

❶ Express the equations in slope-intercept form for graphing.

$$2x - y - 1 = 0$$
$$y = 2x - 1$$
$$-x - y = -5$$
$$y = -x + 5$$

❷ Graph the equations.

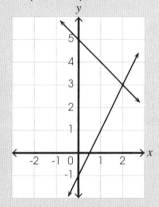

❸ Determine the point of intersection. This is the solution to the equations.

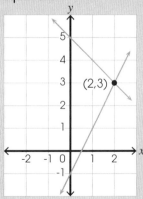

Solution:

$x = 2, y = 3$

㉒ $12 = -x - 2y$ $3x - 4 = 4y$

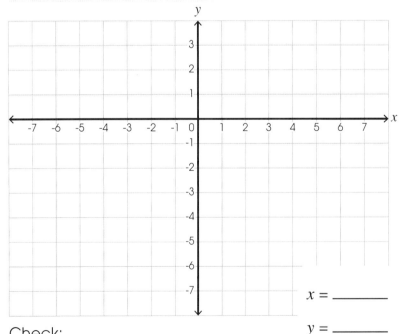

$x =$ _____

$y =$ _____

Check:

Answer the questions.

㉓ Find the point of intersection for each pair of lines graphically.

a. $y = 2x + 1$

$y = 4x + 5$

b. $y = x - 3$

$y = -2x + 3$

c. $y = -x + 5$

$y = \frac{1}{2}x - 4$

d. $y = \frac{1}{3}x - 3$

$y = 3x + 5$

e. $y = -\frac{1}{2}x - 2$

$y = -\frac{3}{2}x - 4$

f. $y = -\frac{2}{3}x - 3$

$y = \frac{2}{3}x + 1$

㉔ Determine whether the lines in each pair have a point of intersection by graphing. If there is, identify it.

a. $y = 2x + 1$

$2x - y = 5$

b. $3y = -x - 6$

$y = -2x + 3$

c. $x - 2y - 2 = 0$

$y = \frac{1}{2}x - 1$

d. $y = -\frac{3}{2}x + 2$

$x + 4y = -12$

e. $y = -4x + 3$

$4x + y + 5 = 0$

f. $5x + y - 4 = 0$

$x - 2y - 14 = 0$

㉕ Determine whether the lines in each pair intersect infinitely without graphing.

a. $y = \frac{2}{3}x - \frac{2}{3}$

$2x - 3y - 2 = 0$

b. $2y = -x - 2$

$y = -\frac{1}{2}x - 2$

c. $x - 3y - 3 = 0$

$y = \frac{1}{3}x - 1$

㉖ Describe how to check whether (-2,-1) is the only point of intersection of $y = 3x + 5$ and $y = -2x - 5$ without graphing.

㉗ Determine whether each point is the point of intersection of each pair of lines algebraically.

a. (-3,-2): $x = -3$ and $y = \frac{2}{3}x - 3$

b. (4,4): $y = -x + 8$ and $y = x$

c. (6,6): $y = \frac{1}{6}x + 5$ and $3x - y = 12$

d. (5,1): $4x + y - 21 = 0$ and $3x + 5y - 20 = 0$

㉘ Can the graphs of two linear equations have exactly two points of intersection? Explain.

M A T H I R L

Determining points of intersection is an important step in triangulation. Triangulation is the process of determining the location of a point by forming triangles with known points. The use of triangulation can be traced back to ancient Egypt and it is believed that the Egyptians had a sophisticated understanding of a triangle and used this knowledge to create phenomenal structures. Nowadays, the applications of triangulation include land surveying, ocean navigation, astronomy, and much more. Scan this QR code to learn more about triangulation.

Chapter 3

3.2 Parallel Lines and Perpendicular Lines

Key Ideas

Parallel lines are lines that do not intersect at any point no matter how far they are extended. They must also have the same slope.

Perpendicular lines are lines that intersect at a right angle. They have slopes that are negative reciprocals and the product of their slopes is always -1.

With the properties of the slopes, parallel lines and perpendicular lines can be identified graphically and also algebraically by examining the slopes from their linear equations.

Symbols for parallel lines and perpendicular lines:

// denotes "is parallel to"

⊥ denotes "is perpendicular to"

Examples

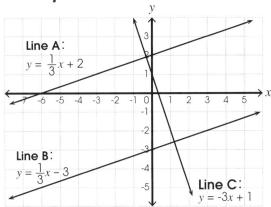

Line A: $y = \frac{1}{3}x + 2$

Line B: $y = \frac{1}{3}x - 3$

Line C: $y = -3x + 1$

Slope of A: $\frac{1}{3}$ ⎤
Slope of B: $\frac{1}{3}$ ⎦ same

Line A and Line B are parallel.

Slope of B: $\frac{1}{3}$ ⎤ negative reciprocals
Slope of C: -3 ⎦ $\frac{1}{3} \times (-3) = -1$

Line B and Line C are perpendicular.

Determine the slopes of the lines. Then identify whether the lines in each pair are parallel, perpendicular, or neither.

① $y = 3x - 2$ $y = 3x + 1$

Slopes: _____ , _____

_____

② $y = -2x$ $y = 2x + 3$

Slopes: _____ , _____

_____

③ $y = \frac{1}{2}x - 1$ $y = -2x + 2$

Slopes: _____ , _____

_____

④ $y = -\frac{1}{3}x + \frac{1}{5}$ $y = -3x + 2$

Slopes: _____ , _____

_____

⑤ $2x + y = -1$ $y = -2x + 5$

Slopes: _____ , _____

_____

⑥ $y = 3x - 7$ $3x + y = 0$

Slopes: _____ , _____

_____

Try these!

Hint

Two lines are neither parallel nor perpendicular when their slopes are different and are not negative reciprocals.

e.g.

$y = x$

$y = -\frac{1}{2}x$

Slopes: $1, -\frac{1}{2}$

The lines are neither parallel nor perpendicular.

For each line, write the slope of a line that is parallel to it and one that is perpendicular to it.

⑦

	Slope of a Parallel Line	Slope of a Perpendicular Line
a. $y = 3x - 5$	_____	_____
b. $y = -2x + 4$	_____	_____
c. $y = \frac{1}{2}x - 5$	_____	_____
d. $y = -\frac{3}{4}x + 1$	_____	_____
e. $3x + 2y = 0$	_____	_____
f. $x - 4y = 3$	_____	_____

Hint

Consider Line A and Line B:

• If Line A // Line B, then
  slope of A = slope of B.

• If Line A ⊥ Line B, then
  slope of A = $-\dfrac{1}{\text{slope of B}}$.

Determine and compare the slopes of the graphs to verify whether they are parallel, perpendicular, or neither.

⑧

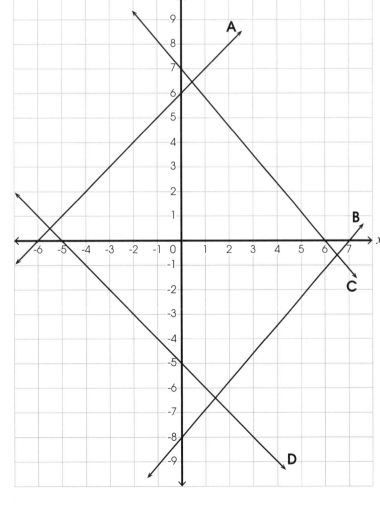

Hint

Determining the relationship of lines solely from their graphs can be inaccurate.

a. Slopes:

• Line A: $\dfrac{\boxed{} - \boxed{}}{\boxed{} - \boxed{}}$ =

• Line B: _____ = ____

• Line C: _____ = ____

• Line D: _____ = ____

b. Relationships:

• Lines A and B: _____

• Lines B and C: _____

• Lines C and D: _____

• Lines A and D: _____

For each line, draw the parallel line and perpendicular line that pass through the indicated point. Then write the equations.

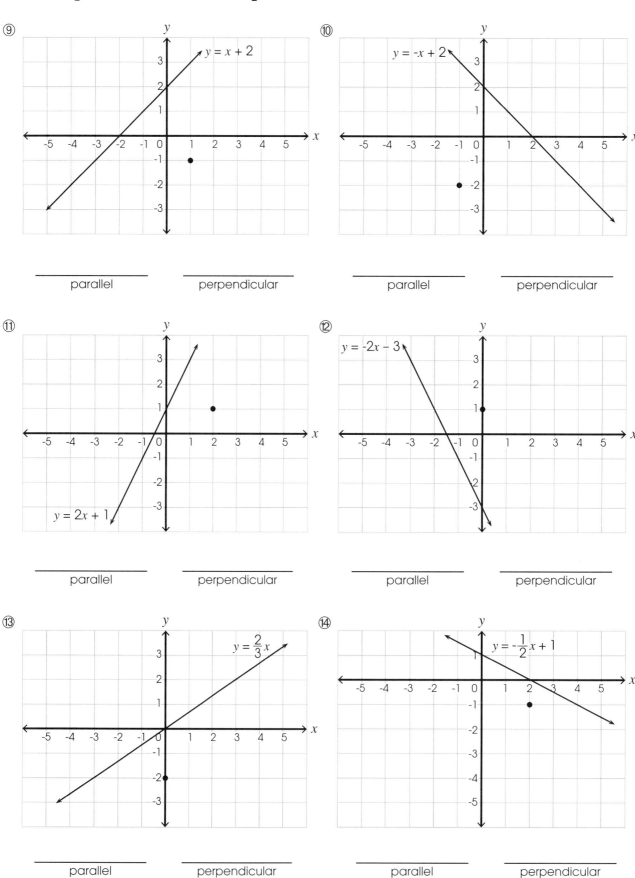

⑨ $y = x + 2$

_____ _____
   parallel   perpendicular

⑩ $y = -x + 2$

_____ _____
   parallel   perpendicular

⑪ $y = 2x + 1$

_____ _____
   parallel   perpendicular

⑫ $y = -2x - 3$

_____ _____
   parallel   perpendicular

⑬ $y = \dfrac{2}{3}x$

_____ _____
   parallel   perpendicular

⑭ $y = -\dfrac{1}{2}x + 1$

_____ _____
   parallel   perpendicular

Plot the points and draw the lines. Determine the equations of the lines. Then identify the parallel lines and perpendicular lines.

⑮

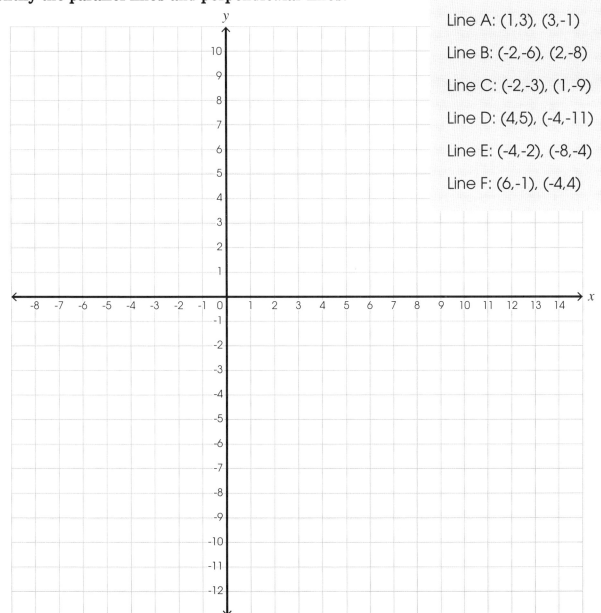

Line A: (1,3), (3,-1)

Line B: (-2,-6), (2,-8)

Line C: (-2,-3), (1,-9)

Line D: (4,5), (-4,-11)

Line E: (-4,-2), (-8,-4)

Line F: (6,-1), (-4,4)

a. Equations of the Lines:

• Line A: _____   • Line B: _____   • Line C: _____

• Line D: _____   • Line E: _____   • Line F: _____

b. Parallel Lines

• Line A // _____

• _____

c. Perpendicular Lines

• Line A ⊥ _____

• _____

• _____

• _____

Find the coordinates of Point Q for each diagram with the given coordinates algebraically. Show your work.

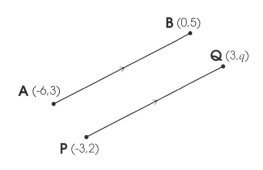

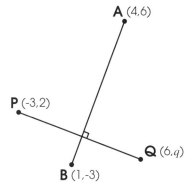

⑯

⑰

① $m_{AB} = $ _____ = _____

② $m_{PQ} = m_{AB} = $ _____

③ Equation of $\overline{PQ}$:

$2 = $ ▨ $(-3) + b$ ← Substitute (-3,2) into $y = \dfrac{1}{3}x + b$.

$b = $ ▨

So, $y = $ ▨ $x + $ ▨

④ Value of q:

$q = $ ▨ $(3) + $ ▨ ← Substitute (-3,q) into $y = \dfrac{1}{3}x + 4$.

$q = $ ▨

Coordinates of Q: _____

For each statement, write T for true and F for false.

⑱ The graphs of $x = a$ and $y = b$ must be perpendicular for any values of a and b. _____

⑲ If $\overline{AB}$ // $\overline{CD}$ and $\overline{AB} \perp \overline{EF}$, then $\overline{CD}$ must be perpendicular to $\overline{EF}$. _____

⑳ If $\overline{AB} \perp \overline{CD}$ and $\overline{CD} \perp \overline{EF}$, then $\overline{AB}$ and $\overline{EF}$ must be perpendicular. _____

㉑ If $\overline{AB}$ // $\overline{CD}$ and $\overline{CD}$ // $\overline{EF}$, then $\overline{AB}$ and $\overline{EF}$ must be the same line. _____

Answer the questions.

㉒ Determine whether the lines in each pair are parallel, perpendicular, or neither.

a. $y = 2x + 1$

$y = -x - \dfrac{1}{2}$

b. $2y = 3x - 1$

$y = -\dfrac{3}{2}x - 2$

c. $2x - y + 1 = 0$

$x - \dfrac{1}{2}y - 3 = 0$

d. $x + y = 2$

$x - y = 4$

e. $y = -\dfrac{1}{2}x - 4$

$\dfrac{1}{2}y = x - 1$

f. $6x - 2y + 4 = 0$

$3x - y - 1 = 0$

㉓ Determine the equation of the line that is parallel to each given line and passes through the given point.

a. $y = 3x - 1$

(-2,-1)

b. $y = x - 5$

(-4,4)

c. $y = \dfrac{1}{2}x + 3$

(10,-1)

d. $y = -2x + 5$

(0,-3)

e. $y = \dfrac{4}{5}x + 2$

(5,2)

f. $y = -\dfrac{3}{4}x - 2$

(-4,6)

㉔ Determine the equation of the line that is perpendicular to each given line and passes through the given point.

a. $y = 4x - 1$

(4,2)

b. $y = -\dfrac{1}{2}x + 2$

(3,4)

c. $y = -3x - 2$

(-6,-1)

d. $y = \dfrac{1}{3}x - 2$

(-2,2)

e. $y = -\dfrac{1}{4}x + 2$

(-1,-4)

f. $y = -\dfrac{2}{3}x - 6$

(-2,1)

㉕ Kyle says, "Every line has only one line that is perpendicular to it." Is he correct? Explain.

㉖ Tommy says that the points A(0,4), B(2,3), C(1,1), and D(-1,2) are the vertices of a square.

a. He says he only needs to find the slopes of the four sides to prove this. Is he correct? Explain.

b. Linda says that she can prove the same using only the slopes of the diagonals. Is she correct? Explain.

㉗ Show that A(-1,5), B(0,2), C(-3,1), and D(-4,4) form a square algebraically.

㉘ Consider A(-2,2), B(5,3), C(-3,-5), and D $(d,-4)$, and $\overline{AB}$ is parallel to $\overline{CD}$.

a. Determine the value of d.

b. Determine whether $\overline{AD}$ and $\overline{BC}$ are perpendicular.

Chapter 3

3.3 Applications of Linear Relations (1)

Key Ideas

Many problems can be modelled by equations and those that involve a constant rate of change can be modelled by linear equations. Linear equations can be solved algebraically or by graphing.

To solve a problem by graphing:

❶ Use variables to represent the unknown values.

❷ Set up the equation.

❸ Graph the equation to obtain the solution.

Remember that it is good practice to write a concluding sentence to state your solution to the problem.

Examples

A coupon booklet that is worth $6 contains either $1 or $2 coupons. Set up an equation to show the number of $1 and $2 coupons.

❶ Let x and y be the number of $1 and $2 coupons respectively.

❷ $x + 2y = 6$ ←— a linear equation that represents the problem

❸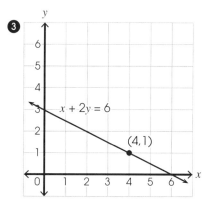

How many $2 coupons are there if there are four $1 coupons?
└ implies $x = 4$

In the graph, when $x = 4$, $y = 1$.

So, there is one $2 coupon.

Try these!

Set up an equation for each scenario. Fill in the blanks.

① Ben made a $2500 investment in stocks. He then bought more stocks at $3/share. How much is his total investment?

Let s be the number of shares bought and i be the total investment.

$$3 \boxed{} + 2500 = \boxed{}$$

② Peppers were sold in packages of 3 or 4. Patrick bought a mix of both packages to get 22 peppers. How many packages of each quantity did he buy?

Let t be the number of packages of 3 and f be the number of packages of 4.

$$3 \boxed{} + 4 \boxed{} = 22$$

③ To rent a lawn aerator, there is a fee of $60 plus $40/day. What is the total cost of rental?

Let d be the number of days and c be the total cost.

$$60 + 40 \boxed{} = \boxed{}$$

④ Dana is a dog walker and walks 4 dogs in 3 hours. She charges an hourly wage plus a pick-up fee of $22. How much does she earn from walking each dog?

Let w be the hourly wage and e be the earning from each dog.

$$3 \boxed{} + 22 = 4 \boxed{}$$

Read each scenario. Check the correct equation and solve the problem by graphing.

⑤ A rectangular chicken pen is built with a perimeter of 14 m. Let x be the length and y be the width.

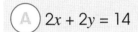 (A) $2x + 2y = 14$ 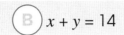 (B) $x + y = 14$

a. If the pen has a length of 4 m, what is its width?

b. If the pen has a width of 2 m, what is its length?

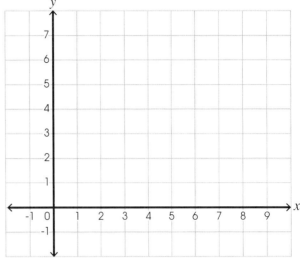

⑥ A stamp collection is worth $30. It contains stamps that are worth either $4 or $5. Let x be the number of $4 stamps and y be the number of $5 stamps.

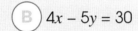 (A) $4x + 5y = 30$ (B) $4x - 5y = 30$

a. If five stamps are worth $4, how many stamps are worth $5?

b. If six stamps are worth $5, how many stamps are worth $4?

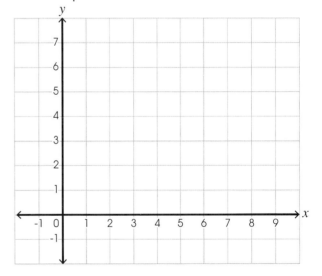

⑦ John bought some $6 mugs with a number of $3-off coupons. He paid $6 in total. Let x be the number of mugs bought and y be the number of coupons used.

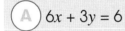 (A) $6x + 3y = 6$ 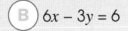 (B) $6x - 3y = 6$

a. If 3 mugs were bought, how many coupons did he use?

b. If no coupons were used, how many mugs did he buy?

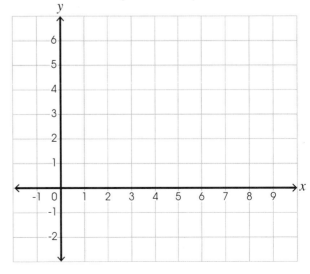

For each scenario, identify the rate of change and the constant. Then match it with the linear equation that represents it. Write the letters.

	Rate of Change	Constant

⑧ **A** The cost of renting a vacuum is $40 plus $3 per day.

_____ _____

B The weight of a container is 3 kg plus machines that weigh 40 kg each.

_____ _____

C A shipment has packages of 40 caps and 3 extra caps as samples.

_____ _____

D A baseball card collection is arranged into 3 equal decks and 1 deck of 40 cards.

_____ _____

Hint

A constant is a value that does not change. The rate of change is the coefficient of a variable, where the change in this variable is relative to the change in another.

e.g. Celsius to Fahrenheit:

$$F = \frac{9}{5}C + 32$$

rate of change (slope)   constant (y-intercept)

$C = 3d + 40$ ◯ ◯ $C = 40d + 3$ ◯ ◯

Check the correct equations and complete the restrictions for the scenarios.

⑨ Sally has $30 in savings and gets an allowance of $5/week, up to 52 weeks.

Ⓐ $S = 30 + 5w$

Ⓑ $S = 30 - 5w$

w (number of weeks) is restricted to whole numbers of _____ or less.

Hint

Any restrictions on the variables in an equation allow for a realistic interpretation of the scenario it models.

e.g. Perimeter of a Square:
$$P = 4s$$
P and s are restricted to positive numbers.

⑩ Tony is a waiter and works 8 hours at an hourly wage, where the minimum wage is $15/h. Today, he received a total of $50 as tips.

Ⓐ $T = 50w + 8$

Ⓑ $T = 8w + 50$

w (hourly wage) is restricted to any value of _____ or greater.

⑪ A train has a capacity of 1000 passengers. Each of the 20 cabins has the same number of passengers after 10 passengers disembarked.

Ⓐ $T = 20p + 10$

Ⓑ $T = 10p - 20$

T (total number of passengers) is restricted to whole numbers up to _____ .

For each scenario, find the restrictions on the variables. Then answer the questions.

⑫ **$F = 25 + 5n$**

F is the promotional entrance fee for a family and n is the number of people in the family. This promotion is valid for families with family size of 2 to 5.

Hint

Substitute the restricted values into the equation to determine the restrictions on the other variable.

Restrictions:

• n: whole numbers from 2 to 5

• F: numbers from _____ to _____

Value of F for $n = 2$:

$F = 25 + 5(2) = $ _____

Value of F for $n = 5$:

$F = 25 + 5(5) = $ _____

⑬ **$R = 1000 - 40m$**

R is the amount of flour remaining in grams and m is the number of muffins baked in a muffin tray that has 12 cups.

Restrictions:

• m: _____

• R: _____

⑭ **$S = 90 - 15e$**

S is the performance score and e is the number of errors up to 6 before getting disqualified.

Restrictions:

• e: _____

• S: _____

⑮ **$y = 3x + 2$**

y is the number of books in an order and x is the number of sets which is limited to 4.

Restrictions:

• x: _____

• y: _____

a. Graph the linear equation.

b. Plot all the possible values of x and y on the graph.

c. Interpret what the plotted points show.

_____

_____

_____

_____

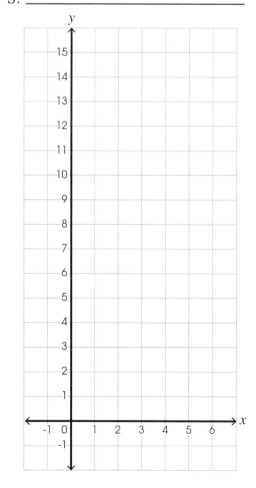

Model each scenario using a linear equation. Graph the equation and answer the questions.

⑯ A sticker book has 24 stickers and consists of pages of either 4 stickers or 6 stickers.

    a. Write an equation to represent the scenario and graph it.

    b. Write the restrictions on the variables.

    c. Identify all the possible number of pages with 4 stickers and 6 stickers.

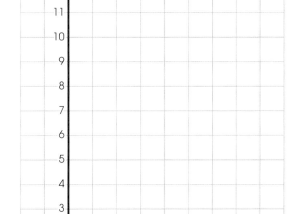

⑰ The retail price of a pair of slippers is $9. Jane had some $1.50-off coupons and she can redeem up to 4 coupons on the slippers.

    a. Write an equation to represent the scenario and graph it.

    b. Write the restrictions on the variables.

    c. Identify all the possible number of coupons used and the amount she paid.

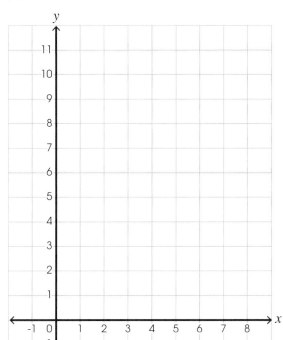

Answer the questions.

⑱ A cash register has $18 in loonies and toonies.

  a. Write a linear equation to represent the scenario.

  b. Determine the restrictions on the variables.

⑲ In the relation $C = 12.5t + 8.5$, C is the total cost and t is the number of tickets sold.

  a. What is the rate of change? What do you think this rate of change represents?

  b. What is the constant? What do you think this constant represents?

  c. If the number of tickets sold is limited to 5, what are the restrictions on the variables?

⑳ Each prize of a lucky draw is either worth $20 or $40 and the total prize of the lucky draw is worth $200.

  a. Write a linear equation to represent the scenario.

  b. Graph the equation.

  c. If there are six $20 prizes, how many $40 prizes are there?

  d. Determine the restrictions.

  e. Determine all the possible solutions.

㉑ A factory manufactures metal rods. Each metal rod has a reinforced base that weighs 150 g plus 30 g for each centimetre in length.

  a. Write a linear equation to represent the scenario.

  b. Determine the restrictions if a rod has a maximum length of 50 cm.

  c. Is it feasible to list all the possible answers? Explain.

㉒ There are some dimes and quarters in a collection that has a total value of $2. Brendon and Jason modelled the scenario as shown below.

- Brendon:

  Let x and y be the number of dimes and quarters respectively.

  $0.1x + 0.25y = 2$

- Jason:

  Let x and y be the number of quarters and dimes respectively.

  $0.25x + 0.1y = 2$

  a. Whose equation models the scenario correctly?

  b. What are all the possible numbers of each coin?

Chapter 3

Key Ideas

In Chapter 3.1, you learned to determine graphically the point of intersection of two linear relations and verified that the point of intersection is also the solution to the equations, meaning the x- and y-values of the point satisfy both equations.

Applying this concept in real-world application is useful in solving problems and examining the relationships among the variables in the relations.

To solve a problem that can be represented by two linear relations:

❶ Set up the equations.

❷ Graph the equations.

❸ Determine the point of intersection. This point of intersection is the solution to the equations.

Examples

126 eggs were packaged into cartons of 12 and 18. There is a total of 8 cartons. How many cartons of 12 and 18 eggs are there?

Let x and y be the number of cartons of 12 and 18 eggs respectively.

$$12x + 18y = 126 \qquad x + y = 8$$

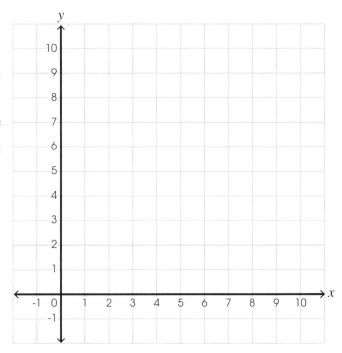

intersect at (3,5); meaning that $x = 3$ and $y = 5$

There are three 12-egg cartons and five 18-egg cartons.

Fill in the blanks to complete the equations. Graph them. Then answer the questions.

Try these!

① Apples are packaged into bags of 10 and oranges are packaged into bags of 12. There are 10 bags of fruits in total with 12 more apples than oranges.

a. Let x and y be the numbers of bags of apples and oranges respectively.

$$10 \quad - 12 \quad = 12$$

$$\boxed{} + \boxed{} = 10$$

b. Point of Intersection: (,   )

c. There are   bags of apples and   bags of oranges.

Write the linear equations and solve the problems by graphing.

② An audiobook subscription service offers two tiers: Tier 1 has a $10 monthly membership fee and charges $0.50/book while Tier 2 has no membership fees and charges $3/book.

 a. Let x be the number of books and y be the monthly cost.

 b. Which plan should Allie choose if she plans to read 3 books this month?

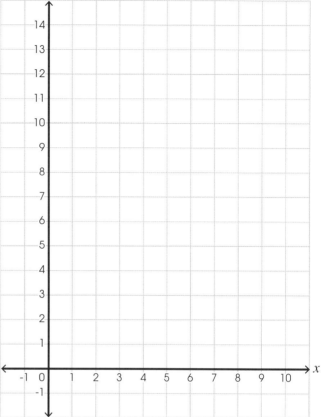

③ Thomas is choosing between two banking services. AAABank has no monthly fees and charges $1.50/transaction. Bank2B has a monthly fee of $6 and charges $0.50/transaction.

 a. Let x be the number of transactions and y be the monthly cost.

 b. At how many transactions will both services cost the same?

 c. Thomas expects to make 10 transactions a month. Which bank should he choose?

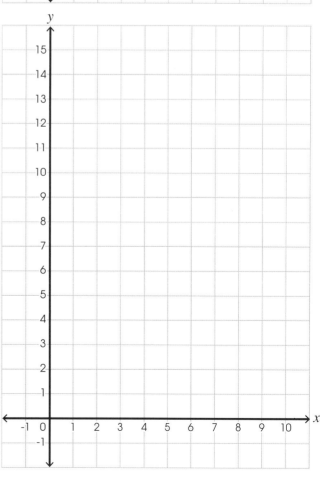

④ Klara started a bracelet business at home. The start-up cost was $6 and it costs $1.50 to make each bracelet. She plans to sell the bracelets for $3 each.

  a. Let x be the number of bracelets and y be the money amount.

  b. How many bracelets does Klara need to sell to break even?

  c. What is the total profit if she sells 6 bracelets?

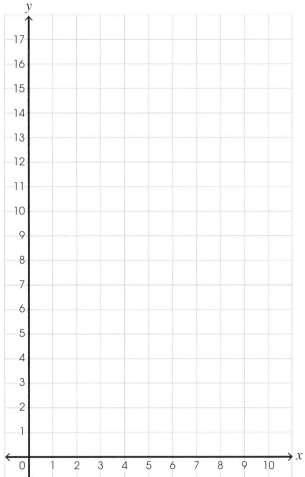

⑤ Johnny goes to two neighbourhoods to raise money for charity. On average, each house donates $4.50 in Green Ravine and $2.50 in Blue Marine. It costs $7 to travel to Green Ravine and $3 to Blue Marine.

  a. Let x be the number of houses and y be the net donation.

  b. Johnny expects at least 10 houses that he visits in either neighbourhood will donate. Which neighbourhood should he go to? Explain.

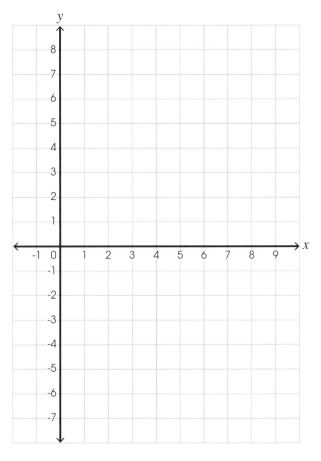

Answer the questions. Use a graphing calculator if needed.

⑥ The owner of a convenience store has bags of chips that are packaged with boxes of 6 bags and boxes of 9 bags. There is a total of 108 bags of chips and 3 more boxes of 6 bags than that of 9 bags.

   a. Write linear equations to model the number of boxes of 6 bags and that of 9 bags.

   b. How many boxes of each number of bags are there?

⑦ For non-members, a courier charges $10 for each delivery. After paying $100 to become a member, the courier charges $5 for each delivery for the year.

   a. Write linear equations to model the costs of delivery yearly.

   b. How many deliveries will make a membership worthwhile?

⑧ To become a babysitter, Lisa took a course which cost $126. As a babysitter, she earns $50/visit and spends $8/visit on transportation.

   a. Write linear equations to model the cost and the income.

   b. After how many visits will babysitting become profitable?

⑨ Storage A has 2100 lamps plus an addition of 300 lamps each month. Storage B has 1500 lamps and 450 lamps are shipped in each month. After how many months will Storage B have more lamps than Storage A?

⑩ A poutine truck has moved its location. Its previous location can sell 30 poutines in one day and costs $250 for parking. Its new location can sell 50 poutines in one day but costs $500 for parking. How much are the poutines sold for if the amount of earnings from both locations are the same? How much is earned each day?

⑪ T.K. is starting an online business selling bookmarks. His competitor sells bookmarks for $3 each and charges a flat rate of $10 for shipping. Create a pricing strategy so that T.K.'s bookmarks are the better buy for orders under $40.

Things I have learned in this chapter:

- determining lines that are parallel, perpendicular, or neither by examining the slopes
- determining the point of intersection of two linear relation
- writing linear equations to model real-life scenarios
- using graphs to solve problems

My Notes:

_____

_____

_____

_____

_____

_____

_____

_____

_____

_____

Knowledge and Understanding

Circle the correct answers.

① If the graphs of two linear equations do not intersect, how are they related?

A. equivalent

B. perpendicular

C. parallel

D. cannot be determined

② Line A and Line B both pass through (0,0) and (2,4). How are the lines related?

A. equivalent

B. perpendicular

C. parallel

D. cannot be determined

③ Consider $x = a$ and $y = b$. What is the point of intersection?

A. (a,b)

B. (b,a)

C. (-a,b)

D. (-b,a)

④ What is the point of intersection of the graphs of $y = x$ and $y = -x$?

A. (1,0)

B. (-1,1)

C. (-1,0)

D. (0,0)

⑤ Which of the following must be the same in parallel lines?

A. x-intercepts

B. y-intercepts

C. slopes

D. all of the above

⑥ What is the product of the slopes of two perpendicular lines?

A. 0

B. 1

C. -1

D. cannot be determined

⑦ The weight in grams of a shipping package of plates is modelled by $W = 150p + 30$, where W is the total weight and p is the number of plates.

a. Which type of numbers can p take on?

A. rational numbers

B. irrational numbers

C. whole numbers

D. integers

b. If p has a maximum value of 6, what is the maximum value of W?

A. 870

B. 900

C. 930

D. no maximum value for W

Identify whether the lines in each pair are parallel, perpendicular, or neither. Then for the pairs of lines that have points of intersection, find the points graphically.

⑧ a. $x - 3y = 3$

$y = \dfrac{1}{3}x - 6$

b. $y = 2x + 1$

$y = -\dfrac{1}{2}x - 4$

c. $2x + y = 1$

$y = 2x - 7$

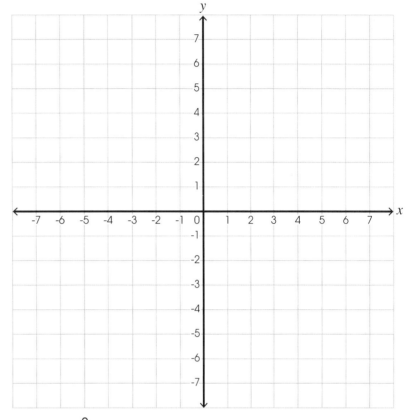

d. $x + 4y = 16$

$y = -2x - 3$

e. $y = -\dfrac{3}{2}x - 4$

$3x + 2y = 8$

f. $4x + 3y = 18$

$4y = 3x - 26$

Draw and write the equation of the lines with the given properties.

⑨

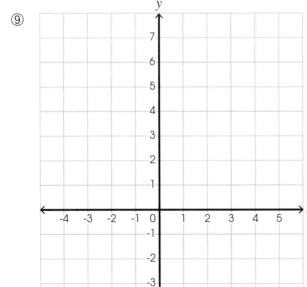

a. Line A: passes through (-4,6) and (-2,5)

b. Line B: parallel to Line A and has a y-intercept of -1

c. Line C: intersects Line A at $x = 0$ and Line B at $y = 1$

d. Line D: perpendicular to Line B and has an x-intercept of 1

Solve the problems by graphing. Show your work.

⑩ A rectangular garden bed has a perimeter of 32 m.

   a. Write a linear equation to model the scenario.

   b. What is the side length if the garden bed is a square?

⑪ Tim bought some drinks sold at $8 each and used some $3-off coupons. He paid $33.

   a. Write a linear equation.

   b. How many coupons did he use if he got 6 drinks?

⑫ Hot dogs are sold for $3 each and hamburgers are sold for $7 each. $91 was made from selling hot dogs and hamburgers.

   a. Write a linear equation.

   b. How many hot dogs were sold if 10 hamburgers were sold?

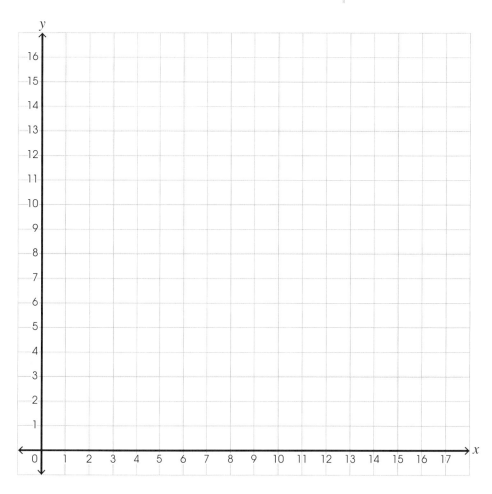

⑬ Blue yarn is sold at $5 plus $0.25/m and red yarn is sold at $1 plus $0.75/m.

　　a. Write linear equations to model the costs of the yarn.

　　b. When is each yarn a better buy?

　　c. What is the price difference at 4 m?

　　d. What are the restrictions?

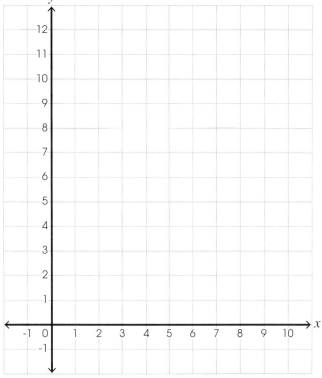

Communication

Answer the questions.

⑭ List all the cases in which two lines can exist in relation to each other.

⑮ "Two parallel lines always have the same slope, but two lines with the same slope are not always parallel." Is this correct? Explain.

⑯ Create a real-life scenario where a variable can take on negative decimal values.

⑰ Describe how you would determine which two lines: $y = \frac{1}{3}x + 2$, $y = -\frac{1}{3}x + 5$, and $x - 3y = -6$, have more than one point of intersection.

Thinking

Find the answers.

⑱ Determine whether the points A(5,7), B(8,2), and C(4,3) form a right triangle without graphing.

⑲ Show that A(2,4), B(3,2), C(-2,-3), and D(-4,1) form a right-angled trapezoid without graphing.

⑳ Two shops sell milkshakes with the option of adding ice cream scoops.

Shop A: Each milkshake costs $3 with an additional cost of $2 for each scoop of ice cream.

Shop B: Each ice cream scoop is $3.

Shop A is the better buy at more than 3 scoops. Find the equation for Shop B and analyze it to suggest a possible selling strategy of Shop B. How much more does a milkshake with 4 scoops of ice cream cost at Shop B than Shop A?

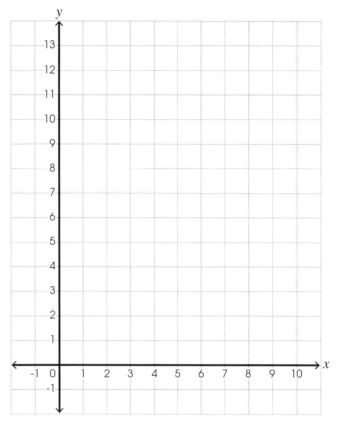

㉑ Power Line A runs straight from (0,7) to (4,1) and Power Line B runs straight from (-6,2) to (-2,-6). A telephone pole is located at (-1,2).

a. Find the shortest distances between the pole and each power line. (Hint: A perpendicular line that passes through the point is the shortest.)

b. Which power line is the telephone pole closer to?

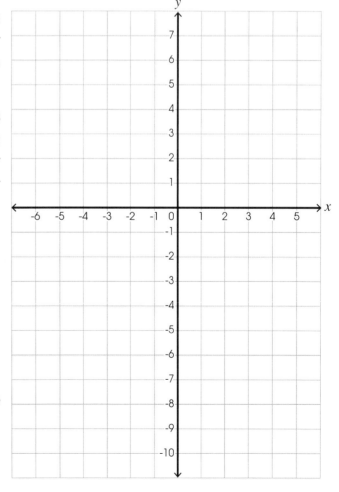

Final Test

Circle the correct answers.

① What is the slope of the line that lies on the x-axis?

    A. 0   B. undefined

    C. 1   D. -1

② Which line passes through (2,-2)?

    A. $y = 2x - 3$ B. $y = -x - 1$

    C. $y = x - 2$ D. $y = -3x + 4$

③ Which line cannot have an x-intercept of -2?

    A. a line with a negative slope   B. a line that is parallel to the y-axis

    C. a line with a slope of 1   D. a line that is the graph of $x = 1$

④ Which is not possible for the graph of a linear equation?

    A. no x-intercept   B. no x- or y-intercepts

    C. no y-intercept   D. same value of x- and y-intercepts

⑤ Which line does not have a slope that has a magnitude of 2?

    A. $2x + y = 5$ B. $x - 2y = 1$

    C. $4x - 2y + 4 = 0$ D. $y = 2x - 9$

⑥ Which set of information is insufficient to find the equation of a line?

    A. one point and slope   B. x-intercept and magnitude of slope

    C. x- and y-intercepts   D. values of A, B, and C in standard form

⑦ What is the slope of a line that is parallel to the graph of $2x - 3y + 1 = 0$?

    A. $\dfrac{2}{3}$ B. $-\dfrac{2}{3}$

    C. $\dfrac{3}{2}$ D. $-\dfrac{3}{2}$

⑧ What is the slope of a line that is perpendicular to the graph of $x + 3y = 2$?

    A. $-\dfrac{1}{3}$ B. $\dfrac{2}{3}$

    C. -2   D. 3

Consider the given points and answer the questions. Show your work.

A(-1,-4)   B(1,2)   C(-3,1)   D(2,5)   E(3,-3)   F(6,-5)

⑨ Find the slopes of the line segments.

a. $\overline{AB}$ b. $\overline{CE}$ c. $\overline{BD}$ d. $\overline{EF}$

⑩ There are two sets of collinear points. Identify the sets and explain how you know they are collinear.

⑪ Consider each line segment that comprises the collinear points.

a. Write the equation of the line that is parallel to each and has a y-intercept of 1. Graph the lines.

b. Write the equation of the line that is perpendicular to each and has a y-intercept of -1. Then graph them.

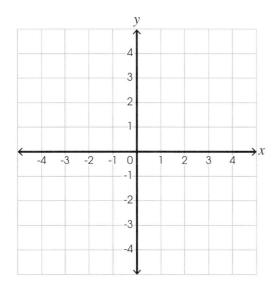

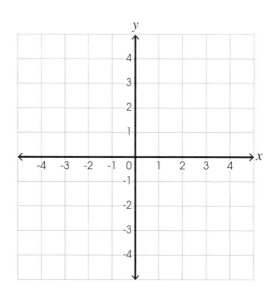

⑫ Indicate the points of intersection in the graphs above. Write their coordinates.   _____

Consider the given linear equations and answer the questions.

⑬

Line A: $y = 5x + 2$ Line B: $x - 5y = -10$ Line C: $y = 2$

Line D: $y = -\dfrac{1}{2}x - 2$ Line E: $5x + y - 2 = 0$ Line F: $5x - y = 0$

    a. Which line that falls from left to right is the steepest?   _____

    b. Which line(s) has/have a y-intercept of -2?   _____

    c. Which two lines are parallel?   _____

    d. Which two lines are perpendicular?   _____

    e. Is (-8,2) a point of intersection of Line C and Line D?   _____

Determine the equation of each line with the given information.

⑭ a line with a slope of -3 and passes through (3,1)

⑮ a line that passes through (-2,2) and has a y-intercept of 5

⑯ a line that passes through (8,5) and (-4,4)

Find the x- and y-intercepts of each line.

⑰ $y = 5x + 5$ ⑱ $x + 2y = -12$ ⑲ $5x - 3y - 15 = 0$

Find the missing values.

⑳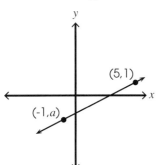

Magnitude of Slope: $\dfrac{1}{2}$

㉑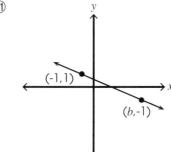

Magnitude of Slope: $\dfrac{2}{3}$

Application

Solve the problems. Show your work.

㉒ The cost of running a private swimming class is modelled by $C = 20s + 300$, where C is the total cost in dollars and s is the number of students, with a maximum of 8.

a. What could the slope and y-intercept of the equation represent?

b. What are the restrictions on the variables?

㉓ Jodie exchanged pack(s) of $3 pens for an $8 stapler and paid a difference for the exchange.

a. Write a linear equation to model the scenario.

b. What are the possible differences she paid?

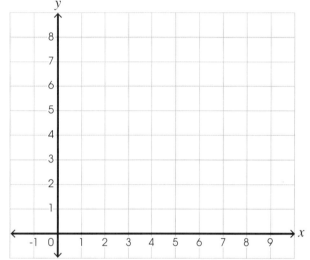

㉔ Apple pies cost $2.50 each and hash browns cost $2 each at a pastry shop. An order of apple pies and hash browns costs a total of $20.   Consider the restrictions and identify the number of each item in the order.

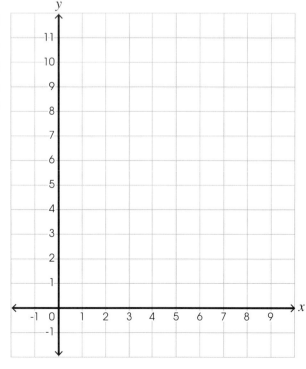

㉕ Podcast A costs $5 plus a charge of $0.75 per episode. Podcast B costs $1 and charges $1.25 per episode.

a. At how many episodes is each podcast a better buy?

b. What is the difference in cost at 4 episodes?

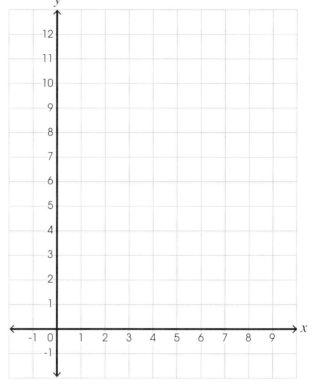

Communication

Answer the questions.

㉖ A linear equation that models a scenario is written in the form of $y = mx + b$. Identify the variables of the equation that represent the rate of change and the constant.

㉗ Describe two similarities and two differences between linear and non-linear relations.

㉘ Describe what the magnitude of a slope is and explain how we determine the steepness of a line by investigating the magnitude of a slope.

Thinking

Answer the questions.

㉙ Find the coordinates that lie on each line.

a. $(a,-a)$ lies on $2x - y - 6 = 0$

b. $(a, \frac{a}{2})$ lies on $y = -\frac{3}{2}x + 8$

㉚ Determine the equation of a line that is parallel to $y = 2x + 5$ and has the same x-intercept as $3x - y + 3 = 0$ algebraically.

㉛ Consider the points A(-1,4), B(3,2), C(2,0), and D(-2,2). The line segments $\overline{AB}$, $\overline{BC}$, $\overline{CD}$, and $\overline{AD}$ form a quadrilateral. Determine what type of quadrilateral is formed without graphing.

㉜ A triangle is formed by Points A, B, and C as shown. Identify the equations of the three altitudes (a line that passes through a vertex and is perpendicular to the side opposite the vertex; the altitude of C is given). Graph the altitudes and find the coordinates of the orthocentre (intersection of the three altitudes).

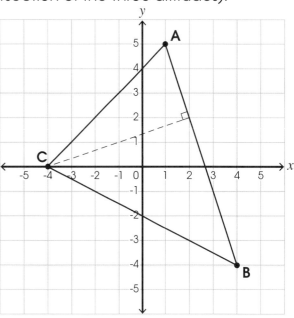

Answers

Chapter 1: Investigating Relations

1.1 The Cartesian Plane

1.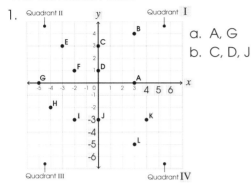

   a. A, G
   b. C, D, J

   c. A: 3 ; 0   B: 3 ; 4   C: 0 ; 3   D: 0 ; 1
      E: -3 ; 3   F: -2 ; 1   G: -5 ; 0   H: -4 ; -2
      I: -2 ; -3   J: 0 ; -3   K: 4 ; -3   L: 3 ; -5

2a. A(3,4)   B(5,6)   C(-2,4)   D(-4,-2)
    E(4,-3)   F(-5,7)   G(-6,-5)   H(0,-3)
    I(-2,0)   J(6,-6)   K(3,-1)   L(-5,-4)

b.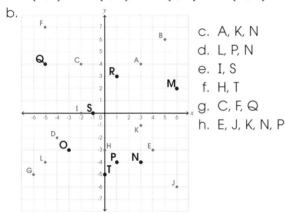

   c. A, K, N
   d. L, P, N
   e. I, S
   f. H, T
   g. C, F, Q
   h. E, J, K, N, P

i. positive ; negative ; positive
   positive ; negative ; negative

3.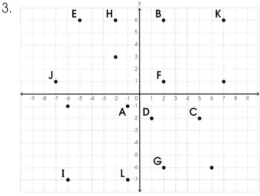

4a. 12 units   b. 3 units

5. Quadrant I: K(7,6) ; B(2,6) ; F(2,1) ; (7,1)
   Quadrant II: H(-2,6) ; E(-5,6) ; J(-7,1) ; (-2,3)
   Quadrant III: A(-1,-1) ; L(-1,-7) ; I(-6,-7) ; (-6,-1)
   Quadrant IV: C(5,-2) ; D(1,-2) ; G(2,-6) ; (6,-6)

6. Set A: L   Set B: V   Set C: Z

7. Set A and Set B

8a.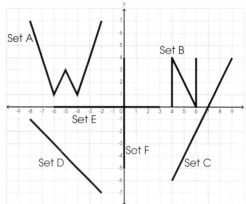

b. Set A forms the letter W. Set B forms the
   letter N. Sets C and D form straight lines.
   Set E lies on the x-axis. Set F lies on the y-axis.

c. (Suggested answers)
   Set A: (-7,4), (-3,4)
   Set B: (4,2), (5,2)
   Set C: (5,-4), (8,2)
   Set D: (-6,-3), (-3,-6)
   Set E: (-2,0), (-1,0)
   Set F: (0,3), (0,0)

9. It is a vertical line.

10. It is a horizontal line.

11. All the points that lie on the x-axis have a
    y-coordinate of 0. All the points that lie on
    the y-axis have an x-coordinate of 0.

12. The parallelogram was reflected.

13. The coordinates of the other two vertices
    are (1,2) and (1,-2).

1.2 Determining the Slope of a Line

1. 10 ; 5   2. 8 ; 4
   3 ; 4   4 ; 3

3. 1 ; 7 ; 1   4. 7 ; 5 ; 3
   1 ; 3   7 ; 2

5a. 4 ; 3 ; 5 ; -5   b. $m = \dfrac{1 - 7}{3 - 1}$
    1 ; 10 $= -3$

c. $m = \dfrac{(-5) - 2}{2 - (-4)}$ d. $m = \dfrac{(-2) - (-3)}{6 - (-2)}$

   $= -\dfrac{7}{6}$ $= \dfrac{1}{8}$

6. $m = \dfrac{9 - 0}{4 - 2}$ 7. $m = \dfrac{5 - 3}{4 - (-1)}$

   $= \dfrac{9}{2}$ $= \dfrac{2}{5}$

8. $m = \dfrac{(-1) - (-3)}{4 - 6}$ 9. $m = \dfrac{(-1) - (-4)}{3 - (-2)}$

   $= -1$ $= \dfrac{3}{5}$

10. $m = \dfrac{(-6) - 1}{5 - 4}$ 11. $m = \dfrac{2 - (-3)}{(-2) - 0}$

    $= -7$ $= -\dfrac{5}{2}$

Answers

12a. $\dfrac{(-6)-3}{4-6}$; $\dfrac{9}{2}$ **b.** $\dfrac{2-3}{(-2)-6}$; $\dfrac{1}{8}$

c. $\dfrac{(-1)-(-6)}{3-4}$; -5   **d.** $\dfrac{(-4)-(-1)}{(-4)-3}$; $\dfrac{3}{7}$

e. $\dfrac{1-(-4)}{2-(-4)}$; $\dfrac{5}{6}$ **f.** $\dfrac{3-(-5)}{6-0}$; $\dfrac{4}{3}$

g. Yes, the slopes should be the same because $\overline{DH}$ and $\overline{HD}$ represent the same line segment.

h. Yes, the slopes of $\overline{AG}$ and $\overline{AC}$ are the same because $\overline{AC}$ is part of the line segment of $\overline{AG}$.

i.

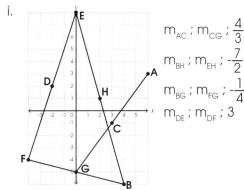

m_{AC} ; m_{CG} ; $\dfrac{4}{3}$

m_{BH} ; m_{EH} ; $-\dfrac{7}{2}$

m_{BG} ; m_{FG} ; $-\dfrac{1}{4}$

m_{DE} ; m_{DF} ; 3

13a. $m = \dfrac{(-3)-0}{0-(-3)}$ **b.** $m = \dfrac{(-2)-4}{0-(-2)}$

$\quad = -1$ $\quad = -3$

c. $m = \dfrac{1-(-3)}{0-(-2)}$ **d.** $m = \dfrac{0-(-3)}{3-0}$

$\quad = 2$ $\quad = 1$

14. $\dfrac{2-(-1)}{1-0}$; 3   **15.** $m_{LM} = \dfrac{0-(-6)}{(-4)-(-1)} = -2$

$\dfrac{(-4)-2}{(-1)-1}$; 3 $\quad m_{MN} = \dfrac{4-0}{(-6)-(-4)} = -2$

$=$ $\quad m_{LM} = m_{MN}$

collinear   collinear

16. $m_{RS} = \dfrac{10-(-3)}{(-1)-2} = -\dfrac{13}{3}$ **17.** $q+1$; $\dfrac{4}{3}$

$m_{ST} = \dfrac{7-10}{0-(-1)} = -3$

$m_{RS} \neq m_{ST}$

not collinear

18. $-3 = \dfrac{t-1}{1-(-1)}$ **19.** $-\dfrac{1}{2} = \dfrac{(-4)-(-1)}{2-c}$

$-3 = \dfrac{t-1}{2}$ $\quad -\dfrac{1}{2} = \dfrac{-3}{2-c}$

$t-1 = -6$ $\quad 2-c = 6$

$t = -5$ $\quad c = -4$

20. $-5 = \dfrac{(-7)-e}{3-1}$ **21.** $\dfrac{2}{3} = \dfrac{(-8)-(-2)}{(-3)-u}$

$-5 = \dfrac{-7-e}{2}$ $\quad \dfrac{2}{3} = \dfrac{-6}{-3-u}$

$-7-e = -10$ $\quad 2(-3-u) = -18$

$e = 3$ $\quad -3-u = -9$

$\quad u = 6$

22. $-\dfrac{5}{4} = \dfrac{8-(-2)}{j-4}$ **23.** $\dfrac{3}{2} = \dfrac{(-11)-(-5)}{(-8)-g}$

$-\dfrac{5}{4} = \dfrac{10}{j-4}$ $\quad \dfrac{3}{2} = \dfrac{-6}{-8-g}$

$5(j-4) = -40$ $\quad 3(-8-g) = -12$

$j-4 = -8$ $\quad -8-g = -4$

$j = -4$ $\quad g = -4$

24a. 1   **b.** -1   **c.** -3   **d.** $\dfrac{2}{5}$

e. $-\dfrac{1}{3}$ **f.** $\dfrac{2}{3}$ **g.** $-\dfrac{3}{4}$ **h.** $-\dfrac{5}{6}$

i. $\dfrac{3}{10}$ **j.** $\dfrac{3}{5}$

25. (7,-1)   **26.** (0,-2)

27a. 1   **b.** -3   **c.** 0   **d.** 6

28. The points in Set A and Set D are collinear. The line segments formed by any two points in each set have the same slope.

29. Yes, she is correct. The order of the points does not matter as long as the order is the same for both the numerator and the denominator.
(Individual example)

30. No, he is incorrect. Two line segments can have the same slope without being on the same line. These are parallel lines.
(Individual example)

31. No, he is incorrect. The two sets of points, Points A, B, C and Points C, D, E only have one point in common and the five points may not be collinear. There is not enough information to determine the relationship between m_{AD} and m_{BE}.

1.3 Properties of Slopes

1a. $m = -\dfrac{3}{2}$ **b.** $m = \dfrac{1}{3}$ **c.** $m = 3$ **d.** $m = -5$

2. $m = \dfrac{(-4)-5}{4-7}$ **3.** $m = \dfrac{(-3)-1}{(-5)-(-7)}$

$\quad = 3$ $\quad = -2$

4. $m = \dfrac{(-4)-4}{8-9}$ **5.** $m = \dfrac{(-3)-3}{3-(-3)}$

$\quad = 8$ $\quad = -1$

6. $m = \dfrac{(-3)-(-5)}{(-2)-(-9)}$ **7.** $m = \dfrac{(-4)-5}{2-1}$

$\quad = \dfrac{2}{7}$ $\quad = -9$

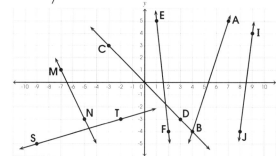

8a. yes　　　　　　　　b. yes
　c. Line EF ; yes　　　d. Line ST ; yes

9a. $m = \dfrac{(-2) - (-2)}{2 - (-7)}$　　b. $m = \dfrac{(-3) - (-4)}{5 - (-4)}$

　　$= \dfrac{0}{9}$　　　　　　　　$= \dfrac{1}{9}$

　　$= 0$

　c. $m = \dfrac{4 - 4}{7 - (-4)}$　　d. $m = \dfrac{(-5) - 5}{4 - 4}$

　　$= \dfrac{0}{11}$　　　　　　　$= \dfrac{-10}{0}$

　　$= 0$　　　　　　　　　$=$ undefined

　e. $m = \dfrac{(-3) - 5}{(-8) - (-8)}$　　f. $m = \dfrac{(-5) - 3}{(-2) - (-6)}$

　　$= \dfrac{-8}{0}$　　　　　　　$= \dfrac{-8}{4}$

　　$=$ undefined　　　　　$= -2$

10. The slopes of the horizontal lines are 0. No, it is not possible because only a horizontal line can have a rise of 0 ($m = \dfrac{0}{\text{run}} = 0$).

11. The slopes of the vertical lines are undefined. No, it is not possible because a vertical line must have a run of 0 ($m = \dfrac{\text{rise}}{0} =$ undefined).

12. Line A:　　　　　13. Line C:

　　$m = \dfrac{(-3) - 4}{(-2) - 1}$　　　$m = \dfrac{(-3) - 3}{1 - (-2)}$

　　$= \dfrac{7}{3}$　　　　　　　　$= -2$

　　Line B:　　　　　　Line D:

　　$m = \dfrac{(-3) - 4}{1 - 4}$　　　$m = \dfrac{1 - (-1)}{2 - (-2)}$

　　$= \dfrac{7}{3}$　　　　　　　　$= \dfrac{1}{2}$

14. The slopes of the parallel lines are the same.

15. The slopes of the perpendicular lines are negative reciprocals.

16a. 3　　　　　　　　b. $-\dfrac{1}{3}$

17a. $-\dfrac{1}{4}$　　b. 4　　c. $\overline{EF}$　　d. $\overline{EF}$

18a. falls　　　　　　b. rises
　c. horizontal　　　　d. vertical
　e. 0 ; m = 0 ; m < 0 ; m = undefined

19a. greater　　　　　b. gentler
　c. parallel　　　　　d. perpendicular
　e. >　　　　　　　f. m_{KL} ; $-\dfrac{1}{m_{MN}}$

20a. $m = \dfrac{3}{2}$　　　　b. $m = -\dfrac{1}{4}$

　c. $m = 0$　　　　　d. $m = -\dfrac{3}{2}$

　e. $m = \dfrac{1}{5}$　　　　f. m = undefined

21a. $m_{AB} = 2$　　b. $\overline{AB}$ and $\overline{GH}$ rise to the right,
　　$m_{CD} = -3$　　　while $\overline{CD}$ and $\overline{EF}$ fall to the
　　$m_{EF} = -\dfrac{1}{3}$　　　right.
　　　　　　　　c. $\overline{CD}$ is the steepest because
　　$m_{GH} = \dfrac{3}{4}$　　　its slope has the greatest
　　　　　　　　　magnitude.

22a. Set A: $m_{MN} = 5$; $m_{OP} = 5$
　　Set B: $m_{MN} = 4$; $m_{OP} = \dfrac{3}{4}$
　　Set C: $m_{MN} = \dfrac{2}{3}$; $m_{OP} = -\dfrac{3}{2}$

　b. The line segments in Set A are parallel because they have the same slope.
　c. The line segments in Set C are perpendicular because their slopes are negative reciprocals.
　d. The line segments in Set B are neither parallel nor perpendicular.

23. The slope of a line that is perpendicular to a vertical line is 0 because the line is horizontal.

24. The slope of a line that is parallel to a horizontal line is 0 because the line is also horizontal.

25. The slope is $-\dfrac{3}{2}$.

1.4　x- and y-intercepts

1a. -3 ; 4　　　b. 2 ; -4　　　c. -1 ; 0 ; 0 ; -2
2a. -2 ; 2　　　　　b. 2 ; -2 ; 1
3a. (-1,0) ; (0,-4)　　b. $\dfrac{(-4) - 0}{0 - (-1)}$; -4

4a. x-intercept: (-4,0)　b. x-intercept: (3,0)
　　y-intercept: (0,6)　　y-intercept: (0,-4)
　　$m = \dfrac{6 - 0}{0 - (-4)} = \dfrac{3}{2}$　　$m = \dfrac{(-4) - 0}{0 - 3} = \dfrac{4}{3}$
　c. x-intercept: (4,0)　d. x-intercept: (-3,0)
　　y-intercept: (0,2)　　y-intercept: (0,-7)
　　$m = \dfrac{2 - 0}{0 - 4} = -\dfrac{1}{2}$　　$m = \dfrac{(-7) - 0}{0 - (-3)} = -\dfrac{7}{3}$

5.

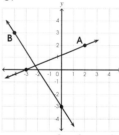

　a. $m = \dfrac{0 - 2}{-3 - 2} = \dfrac{2}{5}$
　b. $m = \dfrac{(-3) - 3}{0 - (-4)} = -\dfrac{3}{2}$

6.

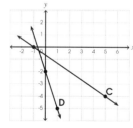

　a. $m = \dfrac{0 - (-4)}{(-1) - 5} = -\dfrac{2}{3}$
　b. $m = \dfrac{(-2) - (-5)}{0 - 1} = -3$

7.

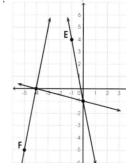

　a. $m = \dfrac{(-1) - 4}{0 - (-1)} = -5$
　b. $m = \dfrac{0 - (-5)}{(-4) - (-5)} = 5$
　c. $m = \dfrac{(-1) - 0}{0 - (-4)} = -\dfrac{1}{4}$

Answers

8a. $0 ; a ; a ; -2 ; -2$ b. $b ; 0 ; b ; 2 ; 2$

9a. $3 = \dfrac{0-6}{a-1}$ b. $3 = \dfrac{b-6}{0-1}$

$a - 1 = -2$ $b - 6 = -3$

$a = -1$ $b = 3$

   -1 3

10a. $-2 = \dfrac{0-(-2)}{a-(-1)}$ b. $-2 = \dfrac{b-(-2)}{0-(-1)}$

$a + 1 = -1$ $b + 2 = -2$

$a = -2$ $b = -4$

   -2 -4

11. $\dfrac{1}{2} = \dfrac{0-(-1)}{a-(-4)}$ 12. $-\dfrac{2}{3} = \dfrac{0-(-2)}{a-6}$

$a + 4 = 2$ $a - 6 = -3$

$a = -2$ $a = 3$

$x\text{-intercept} = -2$ $x\text{-intercept} = 3$

$\dfrac{1}{2} = \dfrac{b-(-1)}{0-(-4)}$ $-\dfrac{2}{3} = \dfrac{b-(-2)}{0-6}$

$b + 1 = 2$ $b + 2 = 4$

$b = 1$ $b = 2$

$y\text{-intercept} = 1$ $y\text{-intercept} = 2$

13. $-\dfrac{5}{2} = \dfrac{0-5}{a-(-4)}$ 14. $m = \dfrac{1-3}{9-3} = -\dfrac{1}{3}$

$a + 4 = 2$ $-\dfrac{1}{3} = \dfrac{0-3}{a-3}$

$a = -2$ $a = 12$

$x\text{-intercept} = -2$ $x\text{-intercept} = 12$

$-\dfrac{5}{2} = \dfrac{b-5}{0-(-4)}$ $\dfrac{1}{3} = \dfrac{b-3}{0-3}$

$b - 5 = -10$ $b = 4$

$b = -5$ $y\text{-intercept} = 4$

$y\text{-intercept} = -5$

15. $m = \dfrac{1-3}{(-5)-5} = \dfrac{1}{5}$ 16. $m = \dfrac{1-(-4)}{(-8)-2} = -\dfrac{1}{2}$

$\dfrac{1}{5} = \dfrac{0-3}{a-5}$ $\dfrac{1}{2} = \dfrac{0-1}{a-(-8)}$

$a = -10$ $a = -6$

$x\text{-intercept} = -10$ $x\text{-intercept} = -6$

$\dfrac{1}{5} = \dfrac{b-3}{0-5}$ $-\dfrac{1}{2} = \dfrac{b-1}{0-(-8)}$

$b = 2$ $b = -3$

$y\text{-intercept} = 2$ $y\text{-intercept} = -3$

17a. $-\dfrac{3}{2}$ b. $\dfrac{2}{5}$ c. $\dfrac{5}{3}$

18a. $(1,0)\ (0,2)$ b. $(-5,0)\ (0,1)$

c. $(-3,0)\ (0,-4)$ d. $(14,0)\ (0,-6)$

19. 3 20. -4

21a. false   b. true   c. true

d. true   e. true   f. false

22a. Quadrants I, II, and III

b. Quadrants I, III, and IV

c. Quadrants II and III

d. Quadrants I and II

23. No. The slope cannot be found if the intercepts are at (0,0).

24. If the slope is positive, it implies that the line rises from the left to the right through (0,0), so it must lie in Quadrants I and III. If the

---

slope is negative, then the line falls from the left to the right and must lie in Quadrants II and IV.

25. The following intercepts are possible: positive x- and y-intercepts, or a positive x-intercept and a negative y-intercept, or a positive x-intercept and no y-intercept.

1.5 Linear Relations and Non-linear Relations

1. 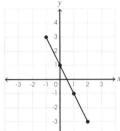   2.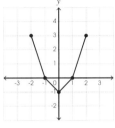

a. $2 ; 2 ; 2$ a. $3 ; 1 ; -1 ; -3$

b. linear   b. non-linear

c. constant   c. not constant

3.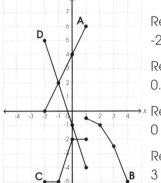

Relation A:
$-2 ; -2 ; -2$

Relation B:
$0.5 ; 1.5 ; 2.5$

Relation C:
$0 ; -3 ; 0$

Relation D:
$3 ; 3 ; 3$

4. The relations that form straight lines when graphed have first differences that are constant. The relations that do not form straight lines have first differences that are not constant.

5. linear   6. linear

7. non-linear   8. $-4 ; -2 ; 0 ; 2 ; 4$
                        $1 ;$ linear

9. $4 ; 1 ; 0 ; 1 ; 4$ 10. $3 ; 2 ; 1 ; 0 ; -1$
   $2 ;$ non-linear $1 ;$ linear

11. $-4 ; -0.5 ; 0 ; 0.5 ; 4$ 12. $2 ; 1 ; 0 ; -1 ; -2$
   $3 ;$ non-linear $1 ;$ linear

Degree of Equation: 1   **Degree of Equation: not 1**

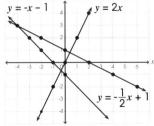   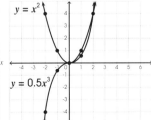

13. Linear relations have a degree of 1. Non-linear relations do not have a degree of 1.
14. degree of 2 ; non-linear
15. degree of 1 ; linear
16. degree of 1 ; linear
17. degree of 2 non-linear
18. degree of 1 linear
19. degree of 2 non-linear
20. 1 ; 1 ; 1
21. -3 ; -1 ; 1 ; 3
22. $\frac{1}{4}$; $\frac{1}{4}$; $\frac{1}{4}$; $\frac{1}{4}$
23. $-\frac{4}{3}$; $\frac{4}{3}$; $-\frac{4}{3}$; $\frac{4}{3}$
24. constant
25. not constant
26. a straight line ; not a straight line
   constant ; not constant
   1 ; not 1
   constant ; not constant
27a. linear ; non-linear
  b. The first differences of Relation A are constant, and the first differences of Relation B are not.
28a. non-linear ; linear
  b. The slopes of the line segments between any two points in Relation D are constant, and the slopes of those in Relation C are not.
29a. linear   b. non-linear
  c. The degree of $y = 4x + 3$ is 1 and the degree of $y = \frac{1}{2}x^2 - 1$ is 2.
30a. Relations A and B are linear, and Relation C is non-linear.
  b. The x-values in Relation B are not evenly-spaced, so determining the first differences cannot be applied.
31a. linear   b. non-linear
  c. non-linear   d. linear
32. No, she is incorrect. A non-linear relation could have two sections with the same slope. It is that other sections of the relation having a different slope that makes it non-linear.
33. No, he is incorrect. Horizontal and vertical lines do not have a degree of 1 but are still linear.

Quiz 1

1. C   2. A   3. D   4. A   5. B
6. B   7. C   8. A   9. T   10. F
11. T   12. T   13. F   14. T

15. $m = \frac{1 - (-3)}{(-2) - (-8)} = \frac{2}{3}$ 16. $m = \frac{4 - (-4)}{5 - 7} = -4$

17. $m = \frac{4 - (-2)}{(-7) - 5} = -\frac{1}{2}$

18a. $m = \frac{0 - (-5)}{(-3) - 0} = -\frac{5}{3}$ b. $m = \frac{0 - (-2)}{5 - 0} = \frac{2}{5}$

c. $m = \frac{0 - (-3)}{(-4) - 0} = -\frac{3}{4}$

19. $m_{AB} = \frac{1 - (-7)}{1 - (-3)} = 2$ $m_{BC} = \frac{7 - 1}{4 - 1} = 2$
   Yes, the points are collinear.

20. $m_{IJ} = \frac{(-1) - 5}{0 - (-2)} = -3$

   $m_{JK} = \frac{(-6) - (-1)}{2 - 0} = -\frac{5}{2}$
   No, the points are not collinear.

21. $m_{DE} = \frac{2 - 0}{0 - (-4)} = \frac{1}{2}$ $m_{EF} = \frac{3 - 2}{3 - 0} = \frac{1}{3}$
   No, the points are not collinear.

22. $m_{PQ} = \frac{4 - 1}{(-6) - 3} = -\frac{1}{3}$ $m_{QR} = \frac{2 - 4}{0 - (-6)} = -\frac{1}{3}$
   Yes, the points are collinear.

23. $\frac{3}{2} = \frac{a - (-5)}{4 - (-2)}$ 24. $-\frac{1}{2} = \frac{b - 1}{(-2) - 4}$
   $a + 5 = 9$ $b - 1 = 3$
   $a = 4$ $b = 4$

25. $m = \frac{0 - 1}{8 - 4}$ 26. $m = \frac{(-1) - 4}{0 - (-1)}$

   $= -\frac{1}{4}$ $= -5$

27. $m = \frac{(-1) - (-4)}{2 - (-4)} = \frac{1}{2}$ 28. $m = \frac{3 - (-2)}{(-6) - 4} = -\frac{1}{2}$
   $\frac{1}{2} = \frac{0 - (-1)}{a - 2}$ $\frac{1}{2} = \frac{0 - (-2)}{a - 4}$
   $a - 2 = 2$ $a - 4 = -4$
   $a = 4$ $a = 0$
   x-intercept: (4,0) x-intercept: (0,0)
   $\frac{1}{2} = \frac{b - (-1)}{0 - 2}$ $-\frac{1}{2} = \frac{b - (-2)}{0 - 4}$
   $b + 1 = -1$ $b + 2 = 2$
   $b = -2$ $b = 0$
   y-intercept: (0,-2) y-intercept: (0,0)

29.

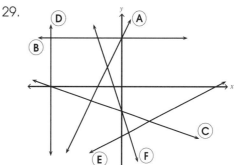

Answers

30. $m_{PQ} = \dfrac{5-(-1)}{(-1)-1} = -3$ $m_{RS} = \dfrac{8-(-4)}{(-4)-0} = -3$

Check if points are collinear:

$m_{PR} = \dfrac{8-5}{(-4)-(-1)} = -1$

The lines are parallel and do not intersect.

31.

x	y
-4	3
0	2
4	-2
8	-3

first differences:

1
4
1

The first differences are not constant. It is a non-linear relation.

32. $m = \dfrac{5-3}{2-7} = -\dfrac{2}{5}$

x-intercept:

$-\dfrac{2}{5} = \dfrac{0-3}{a-7}$

$a - 7 = \dfrac{15}{2}$

$a = 14\dfrac{1}{2}$

The x-intercept is $14\dfrac{1}{2}$.

33. Determine the slopes of the lines. If the slopes are the same, then the lines are parallel. If the slopes are negative reciprocals of each other, then the lines are perpendicular. Otherwise, the lines are neither parallel nor perpendicular.

34. Yes. (4,-5) and (4,3) form a vertical line that cannot pass through (2,m) for any value of m. Therefore, the points are not collinear.

35. - If the first differences are constant, then it is linear.
 - If the degree of the equation is 1 (0 or undefined), then it is linear.
 - If the slopes of any two points in the relation are constant, then it is linear.

36. Slope of the line:

$m = -\dfrac{5}{2}$

Slope of the line segment between (-6,13) and the y-intercept:

$\dfrac{13-(-2)}{(-6)-0} = -\dfrac{5}{2}$

Since the slope of the line segment between (-6,13) and the y-intercept is the same as that of the line, (-6,13) lies on the line.

37. Let a be the value of the x- and y-intercepts.

x-intercept: (a,0)

y-intercept: (0,a)

$m = \dfrac{0-a}{a-0} = -1$

The slope of the line is -1.

38. Since all three points share the same y-coordinate, the line is horizontal. Therefore, the slope of the relation is 0.

Chapter 2: Forms of Linear Equations

2.1 Slope-intercept Form: $y = mx + b$ (1)

1. 2 ; 3   **2.** $\dfrac{1}{2}$; 2   **3.** -3 ; -1   **4.** $\dfrac{3}{4}$; -2

A: $y = 2x + 3$ B: $y = \dfrac{1}{2}x + 2$

C: $y = \dfrac{3}{4}x - 2$ D: $y = -3x - 1$

5. $\dfrac{1}{3}$; 2

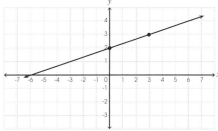

6. $\dfrac{3}{4}$; -1

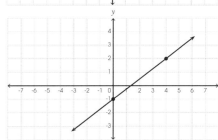

7. $-\dfrac{2}{3}$; 3

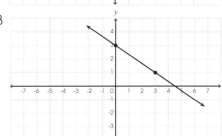

8.   **9.**

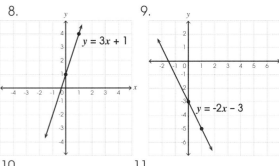

10.   **11.**

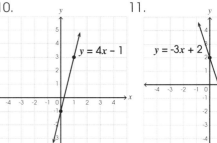

12.

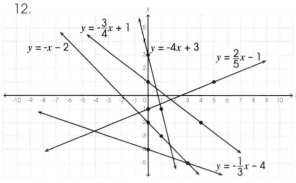

13.

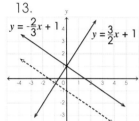

14.

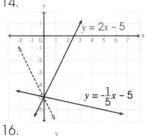

15.

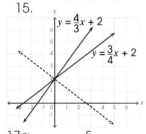

16.

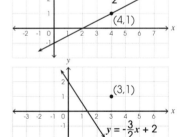

17a. $y = -x - 5$ b. $y = x - 1$

c. $y = -3x + 4$ d. $y = \frac{3}{2}x + 3$

18. $3x - 4$ 19. $-2x + 2$

20. $\frac{1}{2}x + 4$ 21. $-\frac{4}{5}x - 1$

22. $-x + 4$ 23. $11 ; 2 ; 4$
                         $4 ; 3$

24. $m = \frac{(-1) - 2}{2 - 0} = -\frac{3}{2}$ 25. $m = \frac{(-2) - (-4)}{5 - 0} = \frac{2}{5}$

     $y = -\frac{3}{2}x + 2$ $y = \frac{2}{5}x - 4$

26. $m = \frac{(-1) - 5}{8 - 0} = -\frac{3}{4}$ 27. $m = \frac{4 - (-8)}{(-2) - 0} = -6$

     $y = -\frac{3}{4}x + 5$ $y = -6x - 8$

28a. slope $= \frac{4}{3}$, y-intercept $= 2$

b. slope $= -5$, y-intercept $= -2$

c. slope $= -1$, y-intercept $= 3$

d. slope $= 6$, y-intercept $= -4$

e. slope $= 0$, y-intercept $= -2$

f. slope $= -4$, y-intercept $= 0$

29a.

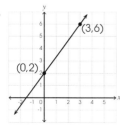

b.

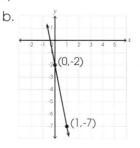

c.

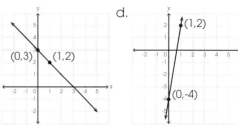

d.

e.

f.

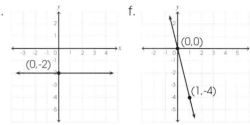

30a. E   b. B   c. A   d. D   e. F   f. C

31a. $y = -\frac{1}{2}x + 1$ b. $y = 2x$ c. $y = \frac{1}{3}x + 2$

d. $y = -4x - 4$ e. $y = -\frac{1}{3}x - 3$ f. $y = \frac{3}{2}x + 3$

32. Yes, $(-3,7)$ lies on $y = -x + 4$.

33. The lines in the form of $y = mx$ all pass through $(0,0)$ and have a y-intercept of 0.

34. No, he is incorrect. The slope of $y = x + 3$ is 1, not 0. Any line with a slope of 1 is not horizontal.

35. Yes, she is correct. The x-coordinate will always be greater than the y-coordinate by 4.

2.2 Slope-intercept Form: $y = mx + b$ (2)

1. $1 ; 4$
    $1 ; 2$
    $1 ; 1$
    lies

2. $1 ; 3$
    $1 = -\frac{9}{2} + 2$
    $1 \neq -\frac{5}{2}$
    does not lie

3. $-5 = \frac{1}{2}(8) - 5$ 4. $-4 = \frac{3}{2}(-4) + 1$

    $-5 \neq -1$ $-4 \neq -5$

    $(8,-5)$ does not $(-4,-4)$ does not lie

    lie on the line.   on the line.

5. $1 = 5(1) - 4$ 6. $12 = -3(-2) + 6$

    $1 = 1$ $12 = 12$

    $(1,1)$ lies on the line. $(-2,12)$ lies on the line.

7. $-8 = -\frac{3}{4}(12) + 1$ 8. $-5 = -\frac{1}{3}(-9) - 8$

    $-8 = -8$ $-5 = -5$

    $(12,-8)$ lies on the $(-9,-5)$ lies on the line.

    line.

Answers

9a. ✔   b. ✔   c. $4 = -(2) + 2$

$4 = 6(2) - 8$ $4 = \frac{1}{2}(2) + 3$ $4 \neq 0$

$4 = 4$ $4 = 4$

10a. $2 = -(-5) - 10$ b. ✔

$2 \neq -5$ $2 = \frac{2}{5}(-5) + 4$

$2 = 2$

   c. ✔

$2 = 2(-5) + 12$

$2 = 2$

11a. ✔   b. ✔

$1 = -4(4) + 17$ $1 = -\frac{5}{4}(4) + 6$

$1 = 1$ $1 = 1$

   c. $1 = \frac{3}{4}(4)$

$1 \neq 3$

12a. $3 = 2a - 5$ b. $b = 2(2) - 5$

$2a = 8$ $b = -1$

$a = 4$

13a. $a = -4(-2) + 5$ b. $b = -4(4) + 5$

$a = 13$ $b = -11$

   c. $33 = -4c + 5$

$4c = -28$

$c = -7$

14a. $a = -\frac{3}{5}(5) - 1$ b. $8 = -\frac{3}{5}b - 1$

$a = -4$ $\frac{3}{5}b = -9$

$b = -15$

   c. $5 = -\frac{3}{5}c - 1$

$\frac{3}{5}c = -6$

$c = -10$

15. $0 = 3x - 3$ $y = 3(0) - 3$

$x = 1$ $y = -3$

x-intercept: (1,0) y-intercept: (0,-3)

16. $0 = -\frac{3}{2}x + 3$ $y = -\frac{3}{2}(0) + 3$

$\frac{3}{2}x = 3$ $y = 3$

$x = 2$ y-intercept: (0,3)

x-intercept: (2,0)

17. $0 = -x - 2$ $y = -(0) - 2$

$x = -2$ $y = -2$

x-intercept: (-2,0) y-intercept: (0,-2)

18. $0 = 2x - 6$ $y = 2(0) - 6$

$x = 3$ $y = -6$

x-intercept: (3,0) y-intercept: (0,-6)

19. $0 = -\frac{1}{4}x + 2$ $y = -\frac{1}{4}(0) + 2$

$\frac{1}{4}x = 2$ $y = 2$

$x = 8$ y-intercept: (0,2)

x-intercept: (8,0)

20. $0 = -\frac{2}{3}x - 6$ $y = -\frac{2}{3}(0) - 6$

$\frac{2}{3}x = -6$ $y = -6$

$x = -9$ y-intercept: (0,-6)

x-intercept: (-9,0)

21a. no   b. yes   c. yes   d. yes

22a. (-8,-7) lies on $y = \frac{5}{8}x - 2$.

   b. (-5,7) lies on $y = 5x + 32$ and $y = -\frac{3}{5}x + 4$.

   c. Since (-5,7) lies on both $y = 5x + 32$ and

$y = -\frac{3}{5}x + 4$, they must intersect at (-5,7).

23a. $a = -6, b = -1$ b. $a = 4, b = -5$

   c. $a = 7, b = 10$

24a. x-intercept = -4   b. x-intercept = 0

y-intercept = -12 y-intercept = 0

   c. x-intercept = 2   d. x-intercept = -9

y-intercept = 1 y-intercept = -6

25. (1,1)

26a. (-12,-12)   b. (4,-4)

   c. (-4,-8)   d. (-36,-24)

27. Yes, he is correct. Any point with a y-coordinate of 3 will satisfy $y = 3$.

28. The linear equation is $x = 5$.

2.3 Standard Form: Ax + By + C = 0

1. $-x$; 8   2. $-3x$; 10   3. $-x + 10$

$-\frac{1}{2}x$; 4 $-\frac{3}{2}x$; 5 $x - 10$

                                 $\frac{1}{2}x - 5$

4. $-2x + 18$ 5. $-2x - 35$ 6. $-3x - 36$

$2x - 18$ $5y$; $2x + 35$ $4y$; $3x + 36$

y ; $\frac{2}{3}x - 6$ y ; $\frac{2}{5}x + 7$ y ; $\frac{3}{4}x + 9$

7. A: $y = -2x + 4$ B: $-2y = -x - 4$

                            $y = \frac{1}{2}x + 2$

   C: $4y = -x - 4$ D: $-5y = -x - 20$

      $y = -\frac{1}{4}x - 1$ $y = \frac{1}{5}x + 4$

   E: $-3y = -4x + 3$

      $y = \frac{4}{3}x - 1$

   B ; E ; A

   C ; D

8. $y = -2x + 3$ 9. $-y = -4x + 1$

-2 ; 3 $y = 4x - 1$

                        4 ; -1

10. $4y = -3x - 4$ 11. $-2y = -x - 4$

$y = -\frac{3}{4}x - 1$ $y = \frac{1}{2}x + 2$

$-\frac{3}{4}$; -1 $\frac{1}{2}$; 2

12. $-5y = -6x + 10$

$\quad y = \dfrac{6}{5}x - 2$

$\quad \dfrac{6}{5}$; -2

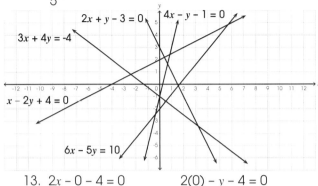

13. $2x - 0 - 4 = 0 \qquad\quad 2(0) - y - 4 = 0$

$\qquad\qquad x = 2 \qquad\qquad\qquad\qquad y = -4$

$\quad$ x-intercept = 2 $\qquad\quad$ y-intercept = -4

14. $x - 2(0) + 8 = 0 \qquad 0 - 2y + 8 = 0$

$\qquad\qquad x = -8 \qquad\qquad\qquad\quad y = 4$

$\quad$ x-intercept = -8 $\qquad\quad$ y-intercept = 4

15. $3x - 4(0) = 12 \qquad\quad 3(0) - 4y = 12$

$\qquad\qquad x = 4 \qquad\qquad\qquad\quad y = -3$

$\quad$ x-intercept = 4 $\qquad\qquad$ y-intercept = -3

16. $3x + 0 + 3 = 0 \qquad\quad 3(0) + y + 3 = 0$

$\qquad\qquad x = -1 \qquad\qquad\qquad\quad y = -3$

$\quad$ x-intercept = -1 $\qquad\qquad$ y-intercept = -3

17. $2x + 3(0) - 12 = 0 \qquad 2(0) + 3y - 12 = 0$

$\qquad\qquad x = 6 \qquad\qquad\qquad\qquad y = 4$

$\quad$ x-intercept = 6 $\qquad\qquad$ y-intercept = 4

18. $x + 5(0) = -5 \qquad\qquad 0 + 5y = -5$

$\qquad\qquad x = -5 \qquad\qquad\qquad\quad y = -1$

$\quad$ x-intercept = -5 $\qquad\qquad$ y-intercept = -1

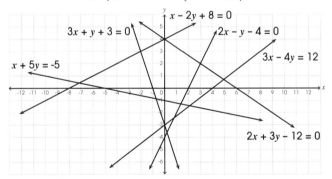

19. $-5x + y + 1 = 0$ $\quad$ 20. $-3x + y - 2 = 0$

$\qquad 5x - y - 1 = 0$ $\qquad\qquad 3x - y + 2 = 0$

21. $\dfrac{1}{2}x + y - 6 = 0$ $\quad$ 22. $-\dfrac{3}{4}x + y + 4 = 0$

$\qquad x + 2y - 12 = 0$ $\qquad\qquad 3x - 4y - 16 = 0$

23. $\dfrac{2}{3}x + y - 2 = 0$ $\quad$ 24. $3x + y - 1 = 0$

$\qquad 2x + 3y - 6 = 0$

25. $-\dfrac{2}{5}x + y + 3 = 0$ $\quad$ 26. $\qquad\qquad y = -\dfrac{3}{2}x - 2$

$\qquad 2x - 5y - 15 = 0$ $\qquad\qquad\qquad \dfrac{3}{2}x + y + 2 = 0$

$\qquad\qquad\qquad\qquad\qquad\qquad\quad 3x + 2y + 4 = 0$

27. $\qquad\qquad y = \dfrac{1}{5}x - 1$

$\quad -\dfrac{1}{5}x + y + 1 = 0$

$\qquad x - 5y - 5 = 0$

28. $\qquad\qquad y = -\dfrac{2}{3}x + 1$

$\quad \dfrac{2}{3}x + y - 1 = 0$

$\qquad 2x + 3y - 3 = 0$

29a. $y = -2x - 1$ $\qquad\qquad$ b. $y = 4x + 2$

$\quad$ c. $y = -\dfrac{1}{3}x + 2$ $\qquad$ d. $y = \dfrac{1}{2}x + 4$

$\quad$ e. $y = \dfrac{3}{4}x + 2$ $\qquad\quad$ f. $y = -\dfrac{2}{3}x + 3$

30a. $x - y + 5 = 0$ $\qquad\quad$ b. $3x - y - 2 = 0$

$\quad$ c. $x - 2y - 6 = 0$ $\qquad$ d. $3x + 5y - 10 = 0$

$\quad$ e. $x - 4y - 3 = 0$ $\qquad$ f. $x + 3y - 2 = 0$

31a. slope: $\dfrac{1}{2}$

$\qquad$ y-intercept: 1

$\quad$ b. slope: -3

$\qquad$ y-intercept: 5

$\quad$ c. slope: $\dfrac{3}{5}$

$\qquad$ y-intercept: 2

$\quad$ d. slope: $-\dfrac{2}{3}$

$\qquad$ y-intercept: 0

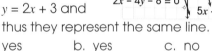

32a. (1,0) and (0,5)

$\quad$ b. (-4,0) and (0,2)

$\quad$ c. (-2,0) and (0,-6)

$\quad$ d. (4,0) and (0,-2)

33. $2x - y + 3 = 0$ can

$\quad$ be rewritten as

$\quad y = 2x + 3$ and

$\quad$ thus they represent the same line.

34a. yes $\qquad\quad$ b. yes $\qquad\qquad$ c. no

$\quad$ d. yes $\qquad\quad$ e. no $\qquad\qquad$ f. yes

35a. $a = -3$ $\qquad\quad$ b. $b = -3$ $\qquad$ c. $c = -2$

$\quad$ d. $d = 6$ $\qquad\qquad$ e. $e = -10$ $\qquad$ f. $f = 7$

36. $m = -\dfrac{A}{B}$, x-intercept $= -\dfrac{C}{A}$, y-intercept $= -\dfrac{C}{B}$

37. $m = -\dfrac{1}{2}$, x-intercept = 4 , y-intercept = 2

2.4 Vertical Lines and Horizontal Lines: $x = a$, $y = b$

1. -2 ; 4 $\qquad$ 2. -1 ; -5 $\qquad$ 3. -3 ; 6

4-7. (Individual points)

$\quad$ 4. vertical

$\quad$ 5. horizontal

$\quad$ 6. vertical

$\quad$ 7. horizontal

$\quad$ 8. Yes, it could be

$\qquad$ determined. If the

$\qquad$ y-coordinate of

$\quad$ the point is the same as the value of y in the

$\quad$ equation, then the point lies on the line.

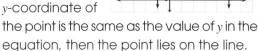

Answers

9. C ; B ; A ; D

10. $x = 1$; $x = 2$; $x = -4$; $x = 5$; $x = 7$
    $y = 3$; $y = -6$; $y = 3$; $y = -2$; $y = 0$

11. (-3,1) $x = 2$ 12. (-1,3) $x = -1$
    (2,-1) $x = -1$ (1,5) $x = 2$
    (-1,3) $y = 1$ (-1,-3) $y = -3$
    (2,3) $y = 3$ (2,-3) $y = 5$

13a. $y = -2$ b. $y = 1$ c. $x = 2$
  d. $x = 3$ e. $x = -1$ f. $y = -4$

14. T   15. T   16. F   17. F
18. T   19. F   20. T   21. T

22a. $x = 3$ b. $y = -5$ c. $x = 2$ d. $y = -3$

23a. (-6,0)   b. (0,-2)   c. (-9,0)
  d. (15,0)   e. (0,7)   f. (0,-8)

24a. Quadrants III and IV
  b. Quadrants I and IV
  c. Quadrants I and II
  d. Quadrants II and III
  e. Quadrants I and II
  f. Quadrants I and IV

25. No, she is incorrect. The x-coordinate of the point, which is a, must be 2 because the point lies on $x = 2$.

26a. (3,-1)   b. (-2,4)   c. (-3,-2)   d. (11,-8)

27a. $x = 2$ and $y = 9$ b. $x = -4$ and $y = 3$
  c. $x = 7$ an $y = -5$ d. $x = -3$ and $y = -4$
  e. $x = 6$ and $y = -1$ f. $x = 0$ and $y = -3$

28. $x = 0$ and $y = 0$

29. $y = mx + b$
    $y = 0x + b$ ← horizontal line (m = 0)
    $y = b$

30. $x = 4$, $x = -2$, $y = 7$, and $y = 3$

31. (5,4), (5,-3), (-2,-3), $x = -2$, $y = 4$

32. A point can only lie on one horizontal line. For a point (a,b), it can only lie on the horizontal line $y = b$. There is not another horizontal line that passes through (a,b) that is not equivalent to $y = b$.

2.5 Equation of a Line

1. 5 ; 1 ; 3
   $m = 5 - 3$
   $m = 2$
   2 ; 3
   2 ; 3

2. 4 ; -3 ; -1
   $b = 4 - 3$
   $b = 1$
   -3 ; 1
   -3 ; 1

3a. $-1 = m(-3) + 5$
    $m = 2$
    $y = 2x + 5$

 b. $3 = m(-1) - 1$
    $m = -4$
    $y = -4x - 1$

c. $-5 = m(4) - 8$
   $-4m = -3$
   $m = \dfrac{3}{4}$
   $y = \dfrac{3}{4}x - 8$

d. $1 = m(5) - 3$
   $-5m = -4$
   $m = \dfrac{4}{5}$
   $y = \dfrac{4}{5}x - 3$

e. $0 = m(16) + 8$
   $-16m = 8$
   $m = -\dfrac{1}{2}$
   $y = -\dfrac{1}{2}x + 8$

4a. $3 = (2)(3) + b$
    $b = -3$
    $y = 2x - 3$

 b. $-6 = (5)(-1) + b$
    $b = -1$
    $y = 5x - 1$

 c. $-3 = (-1)(12) + b$
    $b = 9$
    $y = -x + 9$

 d. $-7 = (-\dfrac{5}{2})(4) + b$
    $b = 3$
    $y = -\dfrac{5}{2}x + 3$

 e. $7 = (-\dfrac{4}{3})(-3) + b$
    $b = 3$
    $y = -\dfrac{4}{3}x + 3$

5. $\dfrac{9 - 1}{(-1) - 3} = -2$
   1 ; -2 ; 3
   $b = 7$
   $-2x + 7$

6. $m = \dfrac{11 - (-1)}{2 - (-1)} = 4$
   $-1 = (4)(-1) + b$
   $b = 3$
   $4x + 3$

7. $m = \dfrac{(-2) - 1}{(-4) - 8} = \dfrac{1}{4}$
   $1 = (\dfrac{1}{4})(8) + b$
   $b = -1$
   $y = \dfrac{1}{4}x - 1$

8. $m = \dfrac{2 - (-4)}{6 - (-3)} = \dfrac{2}{3}$
   $-4 = (\dfrac{2}{3})(-3) + b$
   $b = -2$
   $y = \dfrac{2}{3}x - 2$

9. $m = \dfrac{(-4) - (-1)}{(-6) - (-4)} = \dfrac{3}{2}$
   $-1 = (\dfrac{3}{2})(-4) + b$
   $b = 5$
   $y = \dfrac{3}{2}x + 5$

10. $m = \dfrac{(-10) - (-6)}{5 - (-5)} = -\dfrac{2}{5}$
    $-6 = (-\dfrac{2}{5})(-5) + b$
    $b = -8$
    $y = -\dfrac{2}{5}x - 8$

11. $m = \dfrac{8 - 7}{(-4) - (-2)} = -\dfrac{1}{2}$
    $7 = (-\dfrac{1}{2})(-2) + b$
    $b = 6$
    $y = -\dfrac{1}{2}x + 6$

12. $m = \dfrac{2 - (-2)}{5 - 0} = \dfrac{4}{5}$
    $-2 = (\dfrac{4}{5})(0) + b$
    $b = -2$
    $y = \dfrac{4}{5}x - 2$

13. $11 = m(1) + 9$
    $m = 2$
    $y = 2x + 9$
    standard form:
    $2x - y + 9 = 0$

14. $2 = (-8)(-1) + b$
    $b = -6$
    $y = -8x - 6$
    standard form:
    $8x + y + 6 = 0$

15. $m = \dfrac{(-4) - 2}{(-3) - 6} = \dfrac{2}{3}$ 16. $9 = m(-3) + 5$

$2 = (\dfrac{2}{3})(6) + b$ $m = -\dfrac{4}{3}$

$b = -2$ $y = -\dfrac{4}{3}x + 5$

$y = \dfrac{2}{3}x - 2$ standard form:
standard form: $4x + 3y - 15 = 0$
$2x - 3y - 6 = 0$

17. $-5 = (-4)(3) + b$ 18. $-7 = (-\dfrac{5}{2})(4) + b$

$b = 7$ $b = 3$

$y = -4x + 7$ $y = -\dfrac{5}{2}x + 3$

standard form: standard form:
$4x + y - 7 = 0$ $5x + 2y - 6 = 0$

19. $m = \dfrac{(-3) - 3}{(-10) - (-4)} = 1$ 20. $0 = m(-20) - 10$

$3 = (1)(-4) + b$ $m = -\dfrac{1}{2}$

$b = 7$ $y = -\dfrac{1}{2}x - 10$

$y = x + 7$ standard form:

standard form: $x + 2y + 20 = 0$
$x - y + 7 = 0$

21. $0 = (\dfrac{1}{2})(-6) + b$ 22. $m = \dfrac{(-4) - 0}{(-9) - (-3)} = \dfrac{2}{3}$

$b = 3$ $-4 = (\dfrac{2}{3})(-9) + b$

$y = \dfrac{1}{2}x + 3$ $b = 2$

standard form: $y = \dfrac{2}{3}x + 2$

$x - 2y + 6 = 0$ standard form:

                          $2x - 3y + 6 = 0$

23a. $8 = (2)(2) + b$ 24a. $7 = m(3) - 5$

$b = 4$ $m = 4$

b. $8 = (2)(7) + b$ b. $7 = m(-4) - 5$

$b = -6$ $m = -3$

c. $4 = (2)(-3) + b$ c. $-3 = m(-3) - 5$

$b = 10$ $m = -\dfrac{2}{3}$

25a. $A(-1) + 5 - 2 = 0$ 26a. $(-7) + B(2) + 1 = 0$

$A = 3$ $B = 3$

b. $A(2) + (-12) - 2 = 0$ b. $7 + B(4) + 1 = 0$

$A = 7$ $B = -2$

c. $A(5) + (-18) - 2 = 0$ c. $11 + B(2) + 1 = 0$

$A = 4$ $B = -6$

27a. $2(-1) - 1 + C = 0$ 28a. $3(2) - 2(6) = D$

$C = 3$ $D = -6$

b. $2(3) - 1 + C = 0$ b. $3(-2) - 2(-5) = D$

$C = -5$ $D = 4$

c. $2(-3) - 2 + C = 0$ c. $3(-5) - 2(-3) = D$

$C = 8$ $D = -9$

29a. $y = 3x - 1$ b. $y = \dfrac{1}{2}x + 3$

c. $y = -2x + 8$ d. $y = -\dfrac{3}{2}x - 9$

30a. $x + 3y - 8 = 0$ b. $2x - y + 2 = 0$

c. $3x - 2y - 1 = 0$ d. $x + 4y + 5 = 0$

31a. $m = \dfrac{1}{4}$ b. $b = -5$ c. $A = -\dfrac{1}{4}$ d. $B = 6$

32a. $y = \dfrac{3}{2}x + 3$ b. $y = \dfrac{9}{2}x + 15$

c. $x = -4$ d. $y = 6$

33a. yes   b. no   c. no

34. $y = -2x + 3$, $y = \dfrac{3}{2}x - \dfrac{1}{2}$, and $y = -5$

35. $y = -2x - 2$

36. $y = \dfrac{1}{2}x + 2$

37a. $y = 2$, $y = 6$, $y = 2x + 8$, and $y = 2x - 4$

b. $y = -x + 5$ and $y = \dfrac{1}{2}x + \dfrac{7}{2}$

2.6 Relating Linear Equations

1. 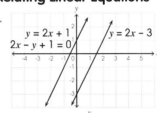   a. different
parallel
b. same
equivalent

2.   a. are
are
b. are not
are not

3. same ; same
equivalent

4. same ; different
parallel

5. same ; different
parallel

6. same ; same
equivalent

7. are
perpendicular

8. are
perpendicular

9. are not
not perpendicular

10. $x + y - 1 = 0 \rightarrow y = -x + 1$
not equivalent

11. $x + 2y + 8 = 0 \rightarrow y = -\dfrac{1}{2}x - 4$; equivalent

12. $3x - 5y + 10 = 0 \rightarrow y = \dfrac{3}{5}x + 2$; equivalent

13. $2x + y = -3 \rightarrow y = -2x - 3$; not equivalent

14. $2x + 2y + 2 = 0 \rightarrow y = -x - 1$
$4x + 2y = -4 \rightarrow y = -2x - 2$
not equivalent

15. $3x + 2y = -4 \rightarrow y = -\dfrac{3}{2}x - 2$

$2x - 3y = 6 \rightarrow y = \dfrac{2}{3}x - 2$
not equivalent

Answers

16. $x - 4y = 4 \rightarrow y = \frac{1}{4}x - 1$

    slopes: $\frac{1}{4}$ and -4 ; negative reciprocals

    perpendicular

17. $2x - y + 3 = 0 \rightarrow y = 2x + 3$

    $4x - 2y = 6 \rightarrow y = 2x - 3$

    slopes: 2 and 2 ; same

    y-intercepts: 3 and -3 ; different

    parallel

18. $x + 2y = 4 \rightarrow y = -\frac{1}{2}x + 2$; equivalent

19. $5x + y = 3 \rightarrow y = -5x + 3$; equivalent

20. $x + 2y - 12 = 0 \rightarrow y = -\frac{1}{2}x + 6$

    slopes: 2 and $-\frac{1}{2}$; negative reciprocals

    perpendicular

21. $x - 4y - 20 = 0 \rightarrow y = \frac{1}{4}x - 5$

    slopes: $\frac{1}{4}$ and $\frac{1}{4}$; same

    y-intercepts: 5 and -5 ; different

    parallel

22a. equivalent   b. equivalent

   c. equivalent   d. not equivalent

23a. parallel   b. not parallel

   c. parallel   d. parallel

24a. not perpendicular   b. perpendicular

   c. not perpendicular   d. perpendicular

25a. equivalent   b. parallel

   c. parallel   d. perpendicular

26a. $y = \frac{2}{7}x - 4$ b. $y = -\frac{7}{2}x + 8$

27. The slopes of the lines must be the same.

28. $A = 2$ 29. $B = 8$

Quiz 2

1. B   2. D   3. D   4. A

5. B   6. D   7. A   8. D

9.

10. $m = \frac{(-1) - 11}{2 - (-2)} = -3$

11. $m = \frac{(-6) - (-5)}{(-6) - 0} = \frac{1}{6}$

12. $m = \frac{(-2) - 5}{2 - 2} = \frac{-7}{0} =$ undefined

13. $m = \frac{(-5) - (-5)}{3 - (-3)} = 0$

14. $m = \frac{(-3) - 1}{(-5) - 5} = \frac{2}{5}$

15. $m = \frac{(-4) - 4}{3 - (-3)} = -\frac{4}{3}$

16. $y = -3x + 5$ 17. $y = \frac{2}{3}x + 3$

    slope: -3   slope: $\frac{2}{3}$

    y-intercept: 5 y-intercept: 3

18. $y = -\frac{1}{6}x + 5$ 19. $6 = (\frac{2}{3})(6) + 6$

    slope: $-\frac{1}{6}$ $6 \neq 10$

    y-intercept: 5   no

20. $-2 = -\frac{1}{4}(-7) - 4$ 21. $3(-2) - 2(-1) = -4$

    $-2 \neq -2\frac{1}{4}$ $-4 = -4$

    no   yes

22. slope-intercept form: $y = -\frac{3}{2}x - 3$

    standard form: $3x + 2y + 6 = 0$

23. $m = \frac{2 - 0}{0 - (-4)} = \frac{1}{2}$

    slope-intercept form: $y = \frac{1}{2}x + 2$

    standard form: $x - 2y + 4 = 0$

24. $m = \frac{(-4) - 2}{1 - 4} = 2$

    $-4 = (2)(1) + b$

    $b = -6$

    slope-intercept form: $y = 2x - 6$

    standard form: $2x - y - 6 = 0$

25. $m = \frac{(-6) - (-1)}{2 - (-8)} = -\frac{1}{2}$

    $-1 = (-\frac{1}{2})(-8) + b$

    $b = -5$

    slope-intercept form: $y = -\frac{1}{2}x - 5$

    standard form: $x + 2y + 10 = 0$

26. $m = \frac{(-1) - (-4)}{2 - (-2)} = \frac{3}{4}$

    $-4 = (\frac{3}{4})(-2) + b$

    $b = -\frac{5}{2}$

    slope-intercept form: $y = \frac{3}{4}x - \frac{5}{2}$

    standard form: $3x - 4y - 10 = 0$

27. $m = \frac{(-3) - 2}{(-2) - (-1)} = 5$

    $2 = (5)(-1) + b$

    $b = 7$

    slope-intercept form: $y = 5x + 7$

    standard form: $5x - y + 7 = 0$

28. equivalent   29. parallel

30. equivalent   31. perpendicular

32. parallel   33. perpendicular

34. $h = 2(-4) + 5$
    $h = -3$

35. $2h + 3(-2) - 2 = 0$
    $2h = 8$
    $h = 4$

36. $7 = h(6) + 4$
    $6h = 3$
    $h = \frac{1}{2}$

37. $2(1) - (-2) + h = 0$
    $4 + h = 0$
    $h = -4$

38. $2(-6) - h(-2) = 6$
    $-12 + 2h = 6$
    $h = 9$

39. $h(-3) - 3(8) + 9 = 0$
    $-3h - 15 = 0$
    $h = -5$

40. $m = \frac{3 - (-1)}{0 - 5} = -\frac{4}{5}$
    The equation is $y = -\frac{4}{5}x + 3$.

41. Yes, it is possible. In order for the line to only lie on Quadrants I and III, the line must pass through (0,0).
    $m = \frac{5 - 0}{6 - 0} = \frac{5}{6}$
    The equation is $y = \frac{5}{6}x$.

42. The equations of the lines are $x = 2$ and $y = -3$.

43. $4x + y - 3 = 0 \rightarrow y = -4x + 3$
    $4x + y = -3 \rightarrow y = -4x - 3$
    He graphed $4x + y - 3 = 0$ and $y = -4x + 3$.

44. One benefit of representing linear equations in slope-intercept form is that the slope and y-intercept are easily identifiable. A benefit of standard form is that it accommodates the horizontal and vertical line equations ($x = a$, $y = b$) in its form.

45. To determine whether two lines are perpendicular, compare the slopes of the lines. If the slopes of the lines are negative reciprocals of each other, then the lines are perpendicular.

46. Use the two points to find the slope. Then substitute the slope and one of the given points into $y = mx + b$ to solve for the y-intercept, b. Then write the equation of the line in slope-intercept form.

47. $-2a = -\frac{1}{2}(a) + 3$
    $-1\frac{1}{2}a = 3$
    $a = -2$
    $-2a = -2(-2) = 4$
    $(a,-2a) = (-2,4)$

48. $a - 5(\frac{1}{4}a) + 3 = 0$
    $a - \frac{5}{4}a = -3$
    $-\frac{1}{4}a = -3$
    $a = 12$
    $\frac{1}{4}a = \frac{1}{4}(12) = 3$
    $(a,\frac{1}{4}a) = (12,3)$

49. $(x,y) \rightarrow (a,a)$
    $a + a - 4 = 0$
    $2a = 4$
    $a = 2$
    (2,2)

50. $(x,y) \rightarrow (a,a)$
    $a - 2a + 4 = 0$
    $-a = -4$
    $a = 4$
    (4,4)

51. $3x - 4y - 4 = 0 \rightarrow y = \frac{3}{4}x - 1$
    slope $= \frac{3}{4}$
    $x + 2y = -4 \rightarrow y = -\frac{1}{2}x - 2$
    y-intercept $= -2$
    $y = \frac{3}{4}x - 2$

52. $0 = -\frac{1}{2}x - 2$
    $x = -4$
    x-intercept: (-4,0)
    $x - 2y + 16 = 0 \rightarrow y = \frac{1}{2}x + 8$
    y-intercept: (0,8)
    $m = \frac{8 - 0}{0 - (-4)} = 2$
    $y = 2x + 8$

53. (3,1) and (-1,1) are 4 units apart. The other possible pairs of points are: (3,5) and (-1,5), or (3,-3) and (-1,-3).
    For points (3,5) and (-1,5), the equations are $x = 3$, $x = -1$, $y = 1$, and $y = 5$.
    For points (3,-3) and (-1,-3), the equations are $x = 3$, $x = -1$, $y = 1$, and $y = -3$.

54. $y = -\frac{2}{3}x + 6$
    $3y = -2x + 18$
    $2x + 3y - 18 = 0$
    $B = 3$

Chapter 3: Interpreting Linear Equations

3.1 Points of Intersection

1-3. (Plot the points of intersection.)
    1. 1 ; 2   2. 1 ; -4   3. -3 ; -4
    4a. (-3,1)   b. (3,-1)   c. (0,-2)   d. (1,3)
    5a. (-4,0)   b. (-5,-5)   c. (0,2)   d. (3,-7)

6.
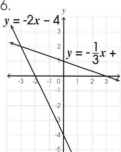
(-3,2)

7.
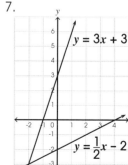
(-2,-3)

Answers

8.

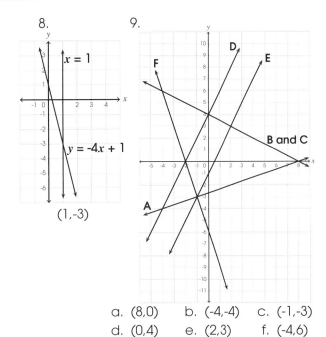

$x = 1$
$y = -4x + 1$
(1,-3)

9.

D
F
E
B and C
A

a. (8,0)   b. (-4,-4)   c. (-1,-3)
d. (0,4)   e. (2,3)   f. (-4,6)

10. No, they do not. They are parallel lines.
11. Yes, they intersect infinitely. They have infinite points of intersection because they are equivalent lines.
12. Three lines intersect at (-1,-3). They are Lines A, E, and F.
13. $-2 = 2(0) - 2$ $-2 = -\frac{1}{2}(0) - 2$
    $-2 = -2$ $-2 = -2$
    (0,-2) is a point of intersection.
14. $4 = -\frac{1}{2}(-4) + 2$ $3(-4) + 4(4) + 3 = 0$
    $4 = 4$ $7 \neq 0$
    (-4,4) is not a point of intersection.
15. intersect at one point ; (1,3)   16. parallel
17. intersect at one point ; (2,-1)
18. equivalent   19. parallel
20. intersect at one point ; (-6,1)

21.

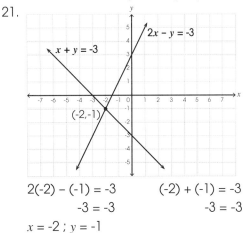

$2x - y = -3$
$x + y = -3$
(-2,-1)

$2(-2) - (-1) = -3$ $(-2) + (-1) = -3$
$-3 = -3$ $-3 = -3$
$x = -2 ; y = -1$

22.

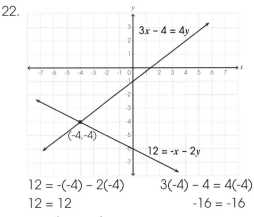

$3x - 4 = 4y$
(-4,-4)
$12 = -x - 2y$

$12 = -(-4) - 2(-4)$ $3(-4) - 4 = 4(-4)$
$12 = 12$ $-16 = -16$
$x = -4 ; y = -4$

23a. (-2,-3)   b. (2,-1)   c. (6,-1)
  d. (-3,-4)   e. (-2,-1)   f. (-3,-1)
24a. no   b. yes ; (3,-3)
  c. yes ; infinite points of intersection
  d. yes ; (4,-4) e. no   f. yes ; (2,-6)
25a. yes   b. no   c. yes
26. Substitute (-2,-1) into both equations to check whether it satisfies them. Then check whether $y = 3x + 5$ and $y = -2x - 5$ are equivalent. If (-2,-1) satisfies both equations and the equations are not equivalent, then (-2,-1) is the only point of intersection.
27a. no   b. yes   c. yes   d. yes
28. No. If two different points both satisfy two linear equations, then the equations are equivalent and intersect infinitely, implying that there cannot be exactly two points of intersection.

3.2 Parallel Lines and Perpendicular Lines

1. 3 ; 3   2. -2 ; 2   3. $\frac{1}{2}$; -2
   parallel   neither   perpendicular
4. $-\frac{1}{3}$; -3   5. -2 ; -2   6. 3 ; -3
   neither   parallel   neither
7a. 3 ; $-\frac{1}{3}$ b. -2 ; $\frac{1}{2}$ c. $\frac{1}{2}$; -2
  d. $\frac{3}{4}$; $\frac{4}{3}$ e. $\frac{3}{2}$; $\frac{2}{3}$ f. $\frac{1}{4}$; -4
8a. 6 - 0 ; 0 - (-6) ; 1   b. neither
    $\frac{0 - (-8)}{7 - 0}$; $\frac{8}{7}$ neither
                                            neither
    $\frac{0 - 7}{6 - 0}$; $-\frac{7}{6}$ perpendicular
    $\frac{0 - (-5)}{(-5) - 0}$; -1
9.

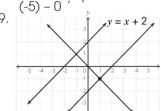

$y = x + 2$
$y = x - 2$
$y = -x$

10.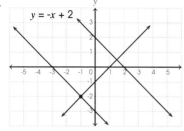

$y = -x - 3$

$y = x - 1$

11.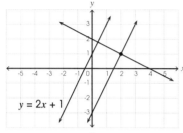

$y = 2x - 3$

$y = -\frac{1}{2}x + 2$

12.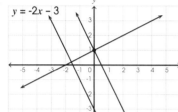

$y = -2x + 1$

$y = \frac{1}{2}x + 1$

13.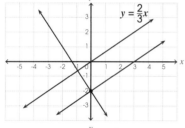

$y = \frac{2}{3}x - 2$

$y = -\frac{3}{2}x - 2$

14.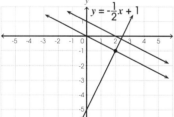

$y = -\frac{1}{2}x$

$y = 2x - 5$

15.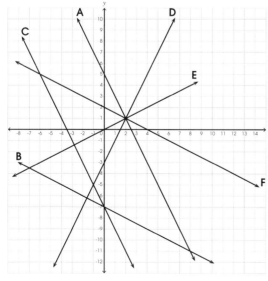

a. $y = -2x + 5$; $y = -\frac{1}{2}x - 7$; $y = -2x - 7$
   $y = 2x - 3$; $y = \frac{1}{2}x$; $y = -\frac{1}{2}x + 2$

b. Line C ; Line B // Line F

c. Line E ; Line C $\perp$ Line E ; Line B $\perp$ Line D ;
   Line D $\perp$ Line F

16. $\frac{5 - 3}{0 - (-6)}$; $\frac{1}{3}$

$\frac{1}{3}$

$\frac{1}{3}$; 3 ; $\frac{1}{3}$; 3

$\frac{1}{3}$; 3 ; 4

(3,4)

17. $m_{AB} = \frac{(-3) - 6}{1 - 4} = 3$

$m_{PQ} - -\frac{1}{m_{AB}} = -\frac{1}{3}$

Equation of $\overline{PQ}$:

$2 = (-\frac{1}{3})(-3) + b$

$b = 1$

So, $y = -\frac{1}{3}x + 1$

Value of q:

$q = -\frac{1}{3}(6) + 1$

$q = -1$

Coordinates of Q: (6,-1)

18. T   19. T   20. F   21. F

22a. neither   b. neither
   c. parallel   d. perpendicular
   e. perpendicular f. parallel

23a. $y = 3x + 5$ b. $y = x + 8$
   c. $y = \frac{1}{2}x - 6$ d. $y = -2x - 3$
   e. $y = \frac{4}{5}x - 2$ f. $y = -\frac{3}{4}x + 3$

24a. $y = -\frac{1}{4}x + 3$ b. $y = 2x - 2$
   c. $y = \frac{1}{3}x + 1$ d. $y = -3x - 4$
   e. $y = 4x$ f. $y = \frac{3}{2}x + 4$

25. No, he is incorrect. There is an infinite number of lines perpendicular to one line. These lines all have a slope that is the negative reciprocal of the line and they intersect with this line at any point.

26a. No, he is incorrect. Finding the slopes of the four sides can check whether the lines are perpendicular. If four pairs of lines are perpendicular, then there are four right angles in the shape. However, a square also has equal sides, which cannot be identified through slopes alone. Even if the four sides form four right angles, the shape can be a rectangle.

b. No, she is incorrect. Finding the slopes of the diagonals can check whether the diagonals are perpendicular, a property which squares have. However, rhombuses and kites also have perpendicular diagonals, so more proof is needed.

Answers

27. Sides:
$m_{AB} = -3$, $m_{BC} = \frac{1}{3}$, $m_{CD} = -3$, $m_{AD} = \frac{1}{3}$
$\overline{AB} \perp \overline{BC}$, $\overline{BC} \perp \overline{CD}$, $\overline{CD} \perp \overline{AD}$, $\overline{AD} \perp \overline{AB}$
Diagonals:
$m_{AC} = 2$, $m_{BD} = -\frac{1}{2}$
$\overline{AC} \perp \overline{BD}$
So, it is a square.

28a. $d = 4$ b. Yes, they are perpendicular.

3.3 Applications of Linear Relations (1)

1. s ; i
2. t ; f
3. d ; c
4. w ; e

5. A

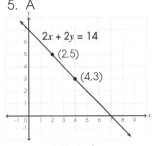

a. Its width is 3 m.
b. Its length is 5 m.

6. A

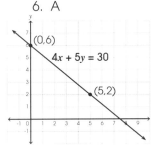

a. Two stamps are worth $5.
b. No stamps are worth $4.

7. B

a. He used 4 coupons.
b. He bought 1 mug.

8. A: 3 ; 40   B: 40 ; 3
   C: 40 ; 3   D: 3; 40
   A ; D ; B ; C
9. A ; 52   10. B ; 15   11. A ; 1000
12. 35 ; 50 ; 35 ; 50
13. m: whole numbers of 12 or less
    R: 520 to 1000
14. e: whole numbers of 6 or less
    S: 0 to 90
15. x: whole numbers of 4 or less
    y: 2 to 14

a-b.

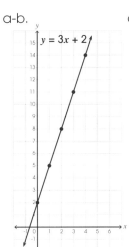

c. In an order, there can be a total of 2 books with 0 sets, 5 books with 1 set, 8 books with 2 sets, 11 books with 3 sets, or 14 books with 4 sets.

16a. Let x be the number of 4-sticker pages and y be the number of 6-sticker pages.
$4x + 6y = 24$

b. x: whole numbers of 6 or less
   y: whole numbers of 4 or less
c. There can be either no 4-sticker pages and four 6-sticker pages, three 4-sticker pages and two 6-sticker pages, or six 4-sticker pages and no 6-sticker pages.

17a. Let x be the no. of coupons redeemed and y be the amount paid.
$y = 9 - 1.5x$

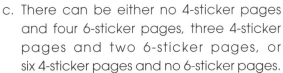

b. x: whole numbers of 4 or less
   y: 3 to 9
c. The possibilities are: no coupons and paid $9, 1 coupon and paid $7.50, 2 coupons and paid $6, 3 coupons and paid $4.50, and 4 coupons and paid $3.

18a. Let l be the number of loonies and t be the number of toonies.

$l + 2t = 18$
b. l: whole numbers of 18 or less
   t: whole numbers of 9 or less

19a. The rate of change is 12.5. This likely represents the cost of each ticket.
b. The constant is 8.5. This likely represents a fixed cost to purchasing the tickets, such as a service fee.
c. t: whole numbers from 1 to 5
   C: 21 to 71

20a. Let x be the number of $20 prizes and y be the number of $40 prizes.

$20x + 40y = 200$

b.

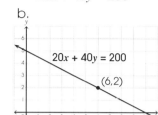

$20x + 40y = 200$

(6,2)

c. There are two $40 prizes.

d. x: whole numbers of 10 or less

y: whole numbers of 5 or less

e. The possibilities are: no $20 prizes and five $40 prizes, two $20 prizes and four $40 prizes, four $20 prizes and three $40 prizes, six $20 prizes and two $40 prizes, eight $20 prizes and one $40 prize, and ten $20 prizes and no $40 prizes.

21a. Let x be the length in centimetres and y be the weight in grams.

$y = 30x + 150$

b. x: numbers from 0 to 50

y: 150 to 1650

c. No, it is not feasible because the length can be a decimal number and there can be infinite possibilities.

22a. Both equations modelled it correctly.

b. The possibilities are: no dimes and 8 quarters, 5 dimes and 6 quarters, 10 dimes and 4 quarters, 15 dimes and 2 quarters, and 20 dimes and no quarters.

3.4 Applications of Linear Relations (2)

1.

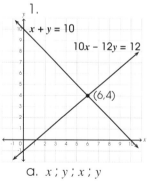

$x + y = 10$

$10x - 12y = 12$

(6,4)

a. x ; y ; x ; y

b. 6 ; 4

c. 6 ; 4

2.

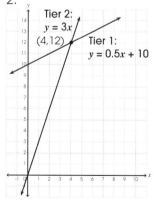

Tier 2:
$y = 3x$
(4,12)

Tier 1:
$y = 0.5x + 10$

a. Tier 1: $y = 0.5x + 10$

Tier 2: $y = 3x$

b. She should choose Tier 2.

3.

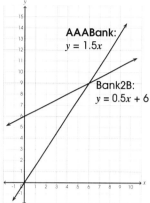

AAABank:
$y = 1.5x$

Bank2B:
$y = 0.5x + 6$

a. AAABank: $y = 1.5x$

Bank2B: $y = 0.5x + 6$

b. Both services will cost the same at 6 transactions.

c. He should choose Bank2B.

4.

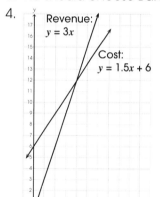

Revenue:
$y = 3x$

Cost:
$y = 1.5x + 6$

a. Cost: $y = 1.5x + 6$

Revenue: $y = 3x$

b. She needs to sell 4 bracelets to break even.

c. $18 - 15 = 3$

The total profit is $3.

5.

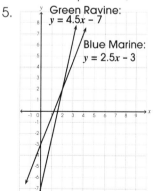

Green Ravine:
$y = 4.5x - 7$

Blue Marine:
$y = 2.5x - 3$

a. Green Ravine: $y = 4.5x - 7$

Blue Marine: $y = 2.5x - 3$

b. He should go to Green Ravine. From the graph, it can be extrapolated that he will collect more donation from 10 houses in Green Ravine than in Blue Marine.

Answers

6a. Let x be the number of boxes of 6 bags and y be the number of boxes of 9 bags.
$6x + 9y = 108$ $x - 3 = y$

b. There are nine boxes of 6 bags and six boxes of 9 bags.

7a. Let x be the number of deliveries and y be the cost of delivery yearly.
Non-member: $y = 10x$
Member: $y = 5x + 100$

b. If the number of deliveries is over 20, it will make a membership worthwhile.

8a. Let x be the number of visits and y be the money amount.
Cost: $y = 8x + 126$ Revenue: $y = 50x$

b. It will become profitable after 3 visits.

9. After 4 months, Storage B will have more lamps than Storage A.

10. The poutines are sold for $12.50 each. $125 is earned each day.

11. (Suggested answer)
He could sell bookmarks at $3.50 each and charge $5 for shipping.

Quiz 3

1. C   2. A   3. A   4. D   5. C   6. C

7a. C   b. C

8.

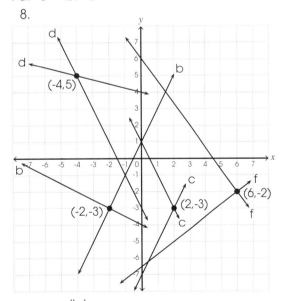

a. parallel
b. perpendicular ; (-2,-3)
c. neither ; (2,-3)
d. neither ; (-4,5)
e. parallel
f. perpendicular ; (6,-2)

9.

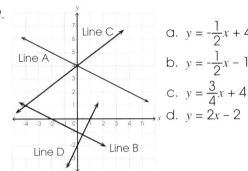

a. $y = -\frac{1}{2}x + 4$
b. $y = -\frac{1}{2}x - 1$
c. $y = \frac{3}{4}x + 4$
d. $y = 2x - 2$

10a. Let x be the length and y be the width.
$2x + 2y = 32$

b. The side length is 8 m.

11a. Let x be the no. of drinks and y be the no. of coupons.
$8x - 3y = 33$

b. He used 5 coupons.

12a. Let x and y be the no. of hot dogs and hamburgers respectively.
$3x + 7y = 91$

b. 7 hot dogs were sold.

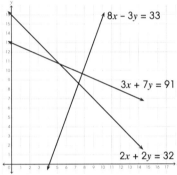

13.

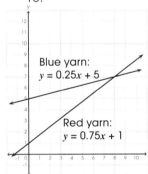

a. Blue yarn: $y = 0.25x + 5$
Red yarn: $y = 0.75x + 1$

b. Blue yarn is a better buy at more than 8 m. Red yarn is a better buy at less than 8 m.

c. The price difference is $2.

d. The length, x, must be greater than 0 (i.e. a positive number). The cost, y, must be at least 5 for blue yarn and at least 1 for red yarn.

14. – equivalent lines that intersect infinitely
– parallel lines that do not intersect
– lines that intersect at one point; those that are perpendicular intersect at 90°

15. Yes, it is correct. Two equivalent lines are the same line with the equations expressed in different forms. They have the same slope but are not parallel line.

16. (Suggested answer)
A variable that represents a stock's value can take on negative decimal values.

17. Lines that have more than one point of intersection are equivalent lines. Equivalent lines have equations expressed in different forms. To identify equivalent lines, convert all equations into the same form.

$x - 3y = -6 \rightarrow y = \frac{1}{3}x + 2$

So, the lines $x - 3y = -6$ and $y = \frac{1}{3}x + 2$ have more than one point of intersection.

18. $m_{AB} = \frac{2-7}{8-5} = -\frac{5}{3}$ $m_{BC} = \frac{3-2}{4-8} = -\frac{1}{4}$

$m_{AC} = \frac{3-7}{4-5} = 4$

$\overline{AC}$ and $\overline{BC}$ are perpendicular, so the points form a right triangle.

19. $m_{AB} = \frac{4-2}{2-3} = -2$ $m_{BC} = \frac{-3-2}{-2-3} = 1$

$m_{CD} = \frac{1-(-3)}{-4-(-2)} = -2$ $m_{AD} = \frac{1-4}{-4-2} = \frac{1}{2}$

$\overline{AB}$ and $\overline{CD}$ are parallel. $\overline{BC}$ and $\overline{AD}$ are not parallel. $\overline{AD}$ is perpendicular to both $\overline{AB}$ and $\overline{CD}$. So the points form a right-angled trapezoid.

20. Let C be the cost and s be the no. of scoops.
Shop A: $C = 2s + 3$
Shop B charges $3 per scoop, so the slope of its graph is 3. It is also given that Shop A is the better buy at more than 3 scoops ($x = 3$), so draw a line with a slope of 3 from the point (3,9).

The equation for Shop B is $C = 3s$. This suggests that each milkshake is free with any scoops of ice cream.

It costs $1 more at Shop B.

21.

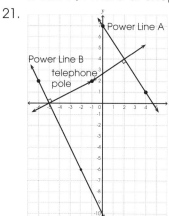

a. Slope of A: $\frac{1-7}{4-0} = -\frac{3}{2}$
Slope of line perpendicular to A: $\frac{2}{3}$
Point of intersection: (2,4)
Shortest distance to A: $\sqrt{2^2 + 3^2} = \sqrt{13}$
Slope of B: $\frac{-6-2}{-2-(-6)} = -2$
Slope of line perpendicular to B: $\frac{1}{2}$
Point of intersection: (-5,0)
Shortest distance to B: $\sqrt{2^2 + 4^2} = \sqrt{20}$

b. It is closer to Power Line A.

Final Test

1. A   2. D   3. D   4. B
5. B   6. B   7. A   8. D

9a. $m_{AB} = \frac{2-(-4)}{1-(-1)} = 3$ b. $m_{CE} = \frac{(-3)-1}{3-(-3)} = -\frac{2}{3}$

c. $m_{BD} = \frac{5-2}{2-1} = 3$ d. $m_{EF} = \frac{(-5)-(-3)}{6-3} = -\frac{2}{3}$

10. The sets of collinear points are: A, B, and D, and C, E, and F. They are collinear because $\overline{AB}$ and $\overline{BD}$ have the same slope and $\overline{CE}$ and $\overline{EF}$ have the same slope.

11a. Set of A, B, and D:
slope = 3
$y = 3x + 1$
Set of C, E, and F:
slope = $-\frac{2}{3}$
$y = -\frac{2}{3}x + 1$

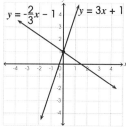

b. Set of A, B, and D:
slope = $-\frac{1}{3}$
$y = -\frac{1}{3}x - 1$
Set of C, E, and F:
slope = $\frac{3}{2}$
$y = \frac{3}{2}x - 1$

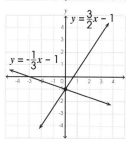

12. (0,1) and (0,-1)

13a. Line E   b. Line D   c. Line A and Line F
d. Line B and Line E   e. yes

14. $y = -3x + b$
$1 = -3(3) + b$
$b = 10$
$y = -3x + 10$

15. $y = mx + 5$
$2 = m(-2) + 5$
$m = \frac{3}{2}$
$y = \frac{3}{2}x + 5$

16. $m = \frac{4-5}{(-4)-8} = \frac{1}{12}$

$y = \frac{1}{12}x + b$

$5 = \frac{1}{12}(8) + b$

$b = \frac{13}{3}$

$y = \frac{1}{12}x + \frac{13}{3}$

17. $0 = 5x + 5$
$5x = -5$
$x = -1$
x-intercept = -1
$y = 5(0) + 5$
$y = 5$
y-intercept = 5

Answers

18. $x + 2(0) = -12$
   $x = -12$
   x-intercept = -12
   $0 + 2y = -12$
   $y = -6$
   y-intercept = -6

19. $5x - 3(0) - 15 = 0$
   $x = 3$
   x-intercept = 3
   $5(0) - 3y - 15 = 0$
   $y = -5$
   y-intercept = -5

20. $\frac{1}{2} = \frac{a-1}{(-1)-5}$
   $2(a-1) = -6$
   $a - 1 = -3$
   $a = -2$

21. $-\frac{2}{3} = \frac{(-1)-1}{b-(-1)}$
   $\frac{-2}{3} = \frac{-2}{b+1}$
   $3 = b + 1$
   $b = 2$

22a. The slope could represent the cost per student. The y-intercept could represent a fixed cost, such as the pool rental cost.

b. The number of students, s, must be a whole number of 8 or less. The total cost, C, must be a number from 300 to 460.

23.
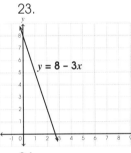
$y = 8 - 3x$

a. Let x be the no. of packs of pens and y be the paid difference.
   $y = 8 - 3x$

b. Jodie exchanged at least 1 pack of pens. The possible differences are $5 and $2.

24.
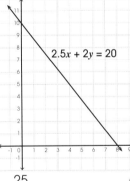
$2.5x + 2y = 20$

Let x be the no. of apple pies and y be the no. of hash browns.
$2.5x + 2y = 20$
x and y must both be whole numbers greater than 0. So, there are 4 apple pies and 5 hash browns in the order.

25.
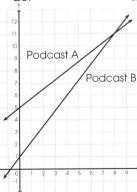
Podcast A
Podcast B

a. Let x be the no. of episodes and y be the total cost.
   Podcast A: $y = 0.75x + 5$
   Podcast B: $y = 1.25x + 1$
   Podcast A is the better buy at more than 8 episodes and Podcast B is the better buy at fewer than 8 episodes.

b. When x is 4, the difference in y is 2. So the difference is $2.

26. m represents the rate of change and b represents the constant.

27. Similarities:
   - shows the relationship between two variables
   - can be modelled using an equation
   Differences:
   - all points on a linear relation are collinear
   - in a non-linear relation, each y-value may correspond to multiple x-values

28. The magnitude of a slope is the numerical value of the slope without any signs. It represents the number of units the slope moves up or down for every unit moved to the right. The greater the magnitude of a slope, the steeper it is.

29a. $2a - (-a) - 6 = 0$
   $3a - 6 = 0$
   $a = 2$
   $(a, -a) = (2, -2)$

b. $\frac{a}{2} = -\frac{3}{2}(a) + 8$
   $\frac{a}{2} + \frac{3a}{2} = 8$
   $a = 4$
   $(a, \frac{a}{2}) = (4, 2)$

30. slope = 2
   x-intercept:
   $3x - 0 + 3 = 0$
   $3x = -3$
   $x = -1$
   $(-1, 0)$

   y-intercept:
   $y = 2x + b$
   $0 = 2(-1) + b$
   $b = 2$

   The equation is $y = 2x + 2$.

31. $m_{AB} = \frac{2-4}{3-(-1)} = -\frac{1}{2}$ $m_{BC} = \frac{0-2}{2-3} = 2$
   $m_{CD} = \frac{2-0}{-2-2} = -\frac{1}{2}$ $m_{AD} = \frac{2-4}{-2-(-1)} = 2$
   $\overline{AB} \perp \overline{BC}$, $\overline{BC} \perp \overline{CD}$, $\overline{CD} \perp \overline{AD}$, $\overline{AD} \perp \overline{AB}$
   Lengths of sides:
   $\overline{AB}: \sqrt{2^2 + 4^2} = \sqrt{20}$ $\overline{CD}: \sqrt{2^2 + 4^2} = \sqrt{20}$
   $\overline{BC}: \sqrt{1^2 + 2^2} = \sqrt{5}$ $\overline{AD}: \sqrt{1^2 + 2^2} = \sqrt{5}$
   length of $\overline{AB}$ = length of $\overline{CD}$
   length of $\overline{BC}$ = length of $\overline{AD}$
   It is a rectangle.

32.
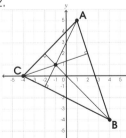

$m_{AB} = \frac{-4-5}{4-1} = -3$
$m_{BC} = \frac{-4-0}{4-(-4)} = -\frac{1}{2}$
$m_{AC} = \frac{5-0}{1-(-4)} = 1$
Altitude of A:
slope of 2 and passes through (1,5)
$y = 2x + 3$

Altitude of B:
slope of -1 and passes through (4,-4)
$y = -x$
Altitude of C:
slope of $\frac{1}{3}$ and passes through (-4,0)
$y = \frac{1}{3}x + \frac{4}{3}$
The orthocentre is at (-1,1).